Just Sell It!

WILEY SMALL BUSINESS EDITIONS

Kim Baker and Sunny Baker, *How to Promote, Publicize, and Advertise Your Growing Business*

Robert A. Cooke, *Doing Business Tax-Free: Perfectly Legal Techniques to Reduce or Eliminate Your Federal Business Taxes*

Fred Hahn, *Do-It-Yourself Advertising: How to Produce Great Ads, Brochures, Catalogs, Direct Mail and Much More*

Daryl Allen Hall, *1001 Businesses You Can Start From Home*

Daryl Allen Hall, *1101 Businesses You Can Start From Home*

Herman Holtz, *How To Start and Run a Writing and Editing Business*

Gregory and Patricia Kishel, *How to Start, Run, and Stay in Business*, Second Edition

John Kremer, *The Complete Direct Marketing Sourcebook: A Step-by-Step Guide to Organizing and Managing a Successful Direct Marketing Program*

Kate Lister and Tom Harnish, *Finding Money: The Small Business Guide to Financing*

Harold J. McLaughlin, *The Entrepreneur's Guide to Building a Better Business Plan: A Step-by-Step Approach*

Richard L. Porterfield, *The Insider's Guide to Winning Government Contracts*

L. Perry Wilber, *Money in Your Mailbox: How to Start and Operate a Mail-Order Business*, Second Edition

Just Sell It!

Selling Skills
for
Small Business Owners

Ted Tate

JOHN WILEY & SONS, INC.

New York • Chichester • Brisbane • Toronto • Singapore

Copyright © 1996 by Ted Tate
Published by John Wiley & Sons, Inc.

Library of Congress Cataloging-in-Publication Data

Tate, Ted.
    Just sell it! : selling skills for small business owners/Ted Tate.
        p.   cm.
    ISBN 0-471-05521-2 (alk. paper). —ISBN 0-471-05688-X (pbk. : alk. paper)
    1. Selling. 2. Small business—Management. I. Title.
    HF5438.25,T38   1996
    658.85—dc20   95-25443
                                                                                         CIP

Printed in the United States of America
10 9 8 7 6 5 4 3 2 1

To:

My sister, Shirley.
My best friend and confidante, without whose help this book
would never have been written.

My daughter, Jennie.
The love and joy of my life and the most thrilling experience
that ever happened to me, in my whole life.

My brother, Bob.
My business partner for many years.
For all the good times and good advice.

My mother, Helen, and father, Ted, Sr.,
who instilled in me from an early age many of the values and
ideas within this book. Gone but never forgotten.

David Morgenstern, my late brother-in-law.
A good man and good friend when I needed one desperately.

Important, please don't skip this page!

This book contains information and personal experiences from the author's lifetime. The author is not, in any way, offering legal, accounting, or other professional advice regarding the matters contained herein.

During my business career I have always made a point of having an attorney and an accountant to whom I could refer for advice. I strongly suggest you do the same. There are simply too many pitfalls and problems that can arise for anyone engaged in selling and/or business. No self-help book in the world can replace the assistance of a competent attorney and accountant.

Good luck and good selling!

Ted Tate
Mentor, Ohio

Contents

Do You Know What Buyer's Remorse Is? / The Art of Getting Sales Referrals

Why Doesn't Everyone Have Goals? / What Goals
Will Do for You / The Easy Way to Set Goals / Goals
Won't Work unless You Really Want Them To

Preface

I gave a motivational speech recently to a large organization. Many members of the audience were highly successful business executives. Most of these men and women had earned their success the old-fashioned American way, one day at a time, starting at, or close to, the bottom.

Being around and speaking with successful people is motivational to me. They inspire me. Their natural enthusiasm for life rubs off on me. Their positive outlook for the future becomes part of me. New ideas and positive thoughts begin to flow.

I always suggest to my students that if they are going to be a success at anything in life, it becomes important that they associate with success, long before achieving it. That means joining organizations to which successful people belong. That means spending leisure time with people who also have dreams and goals to succeed, as you do. That means having the courage to disassociate from negative, sour people who see only the downside.

After my speech to this group, the question-and-answer session turned into a discussion on what was the most desirable trait a person must have in order to succeed in today's tough business world. These top executives had several different views, each backed up by excellent arguments. As we shared ideas, one common thread, one idea surfaced again and again. The trait was persistence: staying with something, not giving up the moment things get tough. The old sayings "talk is cheap" and "actions speak louder than words" tell it it all. It's easy to talk big; it's a lot different when you must go out into the world and back up your talk by doing.

If anything in life separates the failures from the winners most clearly, it's persistence; certainly, in selling any product or service.

Toward the end of this book is a quote from Calvin Coolidge, twenty-third president of the United States, about persistence. If you learn just one thing from this book on selling and small business success, let it be about persistence.

Good luck and good selling!

Ted Tate
Mentor, Ohio

1

Doing It All

THE THRILL OF SUCCESS

If the title of this book got you to the point of reading this page, chances are you are a small businessperson whose sales volume is disappointing. Chances also are that you are looking for a way to correct this situation.

Yet, if you own a small business, you probably already are up to your eyebrows in uncompleted things to do, people to see, and places to go. You are probably hoping for effective ideas that will turn things around and get some real business and cash flow coming in the door.

I have good news: I can help you with that. I've done it before, for myself and for many others, with success. I know how it feels to be sitting alone in a small business, wondering how I can pay bills, wondering what I should do next to bring in business, wondering if I can survive, and knowing I was all alone, that success or failure rested solely in my hands.

Unless you've been there, unless you've taken on those risks and worries by having your own business, you can't possibly understand the pressures your own business can bring. But then again, you can never experience the unbelievable sense of well-being and power you'll feel as you succeed. As your business grows, you know it's because of you. You feel a sense of achievement you've never felt before. Believe me, it's a thrill you never forget.

A Real-Life Example Is in Your Hands Right Now

My dad was in sales most of his life and was a great teacher. I have a lifetime of sales experience, much of it in small business, all successful. I am writing about something I have an expert in-depth knowledge of. I've lived it, I've done it, I believe in it. I know it works. In fact, I know it works big time. I also don't have the slightest doubt that anyone who sincerely follows these strategies will enjoy tremendous success, and that includes you!

One rule I'll discuss with you later is, "If you don't believe that what your business sells will be of benefit to people, find a business that does." Unless you are an outright thief or con artist, you can't sell something you think is of no value or, worse, going to be a bad experience for those who buy from you. I believe in this book, every single word. I want you to believe in what you sell also.

WHO IS THIS GUY?

I've owned and operated several successful businesses in my lifetime. I've also worked as a sales and marketing executive for a few large corporations. I was a partner in and president of a large burglar and fire alarm business that was small when I started with it some 15 years earlier. In every one of those businesses, I was responsible for sales in some manner. In some, I trained salespeople; in others, I managed salespeople; in all, I did at least some of the actual selling, even if I was also managing or training others.

Now I divide my time between two activities: my own business, Tate & Associates, Mentor, Ohio, is a sales training and business consulting firm working with all sizes of businesses to resolve their sales and marketing problems. We do that through personal consulting, seminars, workshops, and giving speeches. Some popular seminar topics include "Power Sales Closing," "How to Double Your Sales," "Successful Negotiation Strategies for Sales and Business Executives," and "Time Management, Personal Motivation, and Goal Setting." My second activity is writing and teaching. This book is a result of that writing. Additionally, I write a monthly column for several national publications on selling and small business topics.

I teach sales and small business courses at a university. In addition to a complete sales course, I also teach two other courses that I have written: How to Market Your Small Business for Success and Selecting and Starting a Small Business from Scratch. I have also developed and market audiocassette tapes on some of these topics. I also just started a line of motivational miniposters, $8\frac{1}{2}$" × 11"; they are large enough to be seen yet small enough to hang in the average office or home workspace. A few of them are quoted in this book. There are several other ideas I'd like to try, but there just hasn't been enough time to get to them—yet.

I must tell you, while this is work, to me it really isn't. I enjoy what I do a great deal and when you enjoy your job, the work becomes pleasurable. I follow my own rules, which you'll be reading about in this book. I honestly believe what I do benefits people in many positive ways. I believe I have assisted many people to make informed, profitable decisions about their businesses and life goals. This book can help you learn the art of selling so that you can improve your business.

WHO SHOULD READ THIS BOOK?

- Small businesspeople who must learn the art of selling to succeed
- Small businesspeople who want eventually to hire others to sell for them
- Individuals considering going into their own small business either full or part time
- Salespeople who sell any product or service
- Sales managers who want new and exciting ways to help their salespeople excel
- Business executives involved in any kind of negotiating, public relations, or sales activity for their company
- New salespeople just starting their careers
- Individuals who are considering a career in selling

THE SMALL BUSINESSPERSON'S DILEMMA

I was teaching a class not long ago on starting up your own business. One fellow mentioned a business he was just about ready to open. I

There are three kinds of people in the world:

Those who **MAKE** things happen

Those who **WATCH** things happen

Those who **WONDER** what happened

said, "You'll need to brush up on your selling skills. That business does best with direct sales calls."

"Oh, I'm not worried," he responded casually. "I'll just pick up a couple of salespeople when I'm ready and just pay them a commission. They'll sell. If they don't, they won't eat. Ha ha."

His appalling statement suggested to me he had little knowledge of business or hiring salespeople, let alone any sensitivity for his fellow humans. Anyone who thinks they can just "pick up" salespeople when they need them, sort of like picking up a quart of milk at the store, is very wrong.

Salespeople, that is, the ones who can really sell, are a valuable commodity. I say the ones who can sell because there are many people who will answer ads for salespeople who really don't have a clue what sales are all about. People who work in retail stores, answer telephones at an order desk in a company, and many others think they are salespeople. I disagree. They may be good order takers and decent human beings, but in my mind, they are not salespeople.

When I speak of salespeople I mean people who can go out on their own; find, develop, and qualify prospects on their own; make a complete sales presentation; and then close a sale. That's a tall order to fill. Talk to executives in any large company that employs large sales staffs. They'll tell you how hard it is to recruit people who really will go out and sell.

If it's that hard for larger firms with strong financial resources to find good salespeople who can and will sell, then where does the small businessperson fit in? At the bottom of the desirability ladder in the eyes of potential sales recruits.

Put yourself in the shoes of someone who is seeking employment. Chances are he or she has a family, financial obligations, and a desire for job security. He or she will be doing everything possible to find employment where at least health benefits are available, where perhaps a retirement plan and possibly a car, or at least a car allowance, are available. This person will also be looking at prospective employers for job stability. Often, to hire good salespeople a company has to put up some sort of salary or guaranteed draw against commission.

If you own a small business, how do you measure up to that standard? Even if you can afford those perks to start, how long can you continue if the salesperson has a slow start or doesn't work out after several weeks and you have to hire another?

When potential salespeople come in for an interview, does your business give the impression of success and stability? Or is it just you, working from a corner of your home, trying to meet people at restaurants for coffee so they don't see where you work? Or do you have a small business location with just a few employees (or worse, relatives) working there?

Keep in mind, talented salespeople have no trouble finding a good job. Once they find one they tend to stay put; they are not in the marketplace very long or very frequently. What about all those people answering ads for sales jobs? A few are good salespeople who for one reason or another are floating around, seeking employment. Many, however, are losers who go from job to job—people who don't know what they want, people who aspire to be in sales, and, finally, people who will take any job available.

How about all those jobs in the paper offering straight commission? Those jobs are very difficult for employers to fill. That's why you see so many commission ads and see the same companies advertising week after week, year after year. Often, they are selling something that has a high rate of rejection and they turn over salespeople at a rapid pace. Most times they settle for less-than-desirable candidates.

The reason straight commissions work is that there are highly skilled sales management people who know how to get maximum results from minimal candidates. The majority of management's time and efforts are focused on recruiting new people every few weeks and squeezing a few sales out of them before they become discouraged and quit. Hiring people on straight commissions is a hard grind and unless you've done it before with success, it's not the way to build a small business.

So what is the answer for the small businessperson? You. You are the answer. You do the selling. I can hear some people saying, "But I don't have the time. I can't run the business and sell, it's just too much!" I can hear others saying, "I just want to manage the business, not sell. I don't like to sell. That's not what I do best."

This is the small businessperson's dilemma. When it's done right, selling takes time. And without new business coming in on a regular basis you lose your business, or, worse yet, you make just enough barely to survive but never grow past that stage—suffering a lifetime of constant struggle just to survive, always paying bills just in time to avoid something being shut off, not taking a salary one week to pay back taxes. That's an ugly way to live your life, yet I know of many, many small businesses doing just that.

Selling Today Doesn't Mean Forever

When I suggest you sell, I don't necessarily mean you do it forever. Once your business starts to succeed, you'll be attractive to the kind of quality salespeople who are well worth the time and effort to hire, train, and supervise.

However, I must warn you that selling is addictive. It's easy to get hooked. Once you experience your first sale, the natural high is unbelievable. There is nothing to compare it with. It's a feeling of power, of success, and will build your self-esteem like crazy!

I told you I was president of an alarm firm. I had enough duties to keep me busy 12 hours a day, seven days a week. Without effective time management I would have burned out my first year. Yet I always had time set aside to sell—not a lot, but I did make some time.

I remember one morning driving to work around 7:00 A.M. I pulled up to a small convenience store, part of a large chain, where I purchased milk every morning for my coffee. This morning a bunch of police cars were there, some with lights flashing.

When I went in I learned that they had just had an armed burglary. I walked up to the manager and said, "I know this is a bad time, but I want you to know there are deterrents to this kind of crime. You're really lucky no one was shot." He took the card I offered and mumbled something about, "I'll let the office know."

I had the feeling it was a wasted effort, but I knew from past experience that most sales calls are. It's simply the law of averages that often separate the average from the truly great salespeople.

Around 10:00 A.M. that morning I got a call from the Security Director of the company that owned the store chain. "I've got your card from our manager. I just thought if you have any literature on your products you could send it to my attention." As you'll learn later in this book, sending literature and waiting for people to respond is a real dead-end street.

Understand, the request from the Security Director was sincere. It's just that literature can't sell because it only deals with hard facts, technical information. Nobody cares about or buys because of that. As you'll learn in this book, people buy from emotion, to solve problems. I knew I needed to see the Security Director so I could help him find realistic solutions to his problem.

"I'll see what I have," I said. "Tell me a little about your problems so I have an idea of what makes sense for your situation." A little? He spoke for over 45 minutes regarding a whole series of crime problems his employer was experiencing. I took notes like crazy, saying very little except to encourage him when he started to slow down. I also qualified that he was the sole decision maker when it came to purchasing security for his firm. When I suggested a meeting, I was thinking of one day the following week. He said that afternoon would be just fine. In fact, what was I doing for lunch?

The bottom line to this story is I sold the chain of 30-some stores protection devices. They were so pleased with the results we also started doing business with their parent company. Over the next several years we did many thousands of dollars in business, all from handing my business card to a potential "suspect."

Most of the time you hand out your card, nothing happens. What I am sharing with you is the exception that makes all the other times worth the effort.

If you believe you can do a thing...

or if you believe you cannot...

you are right.

Henry Ford

As I've mentioned, my dad was also in sales for most of his life. He used to tell me, "You never really know who is going to turn into a customer. Be careful not to judge too quickly until you can ask some qualifying questions. What may not appear on the surface to be a good prospect may be a great one, while the one you think is a natural may never buy anything from you."

SUCCESSFULLY EARNING A LIVING AND KEEPING YOUR SANITY

So how do you do it? How do you sell and run a business at the same time? There are three answers to this question.

1. *Set Your Goals and Use Time Management to Get There.* I've set aside Chapters 13 and 14 just for this purpose. Once you've read them and applied a few of the suggestions, I think this issue will be a lot clearer.

2. *Get Past Any Fears You May Harbor about Selling.* If selling is a new concept to you, the idea of calling on and selling to total strangers can be intimidating. This discomfort, or fear, for some is caused by self-esteem issues, which we'll discuss later, and also about being assertive. I promise you, there are solutions.

3. *Learn to Do It Right.* If you are going to sell, this book will show you a whole series of strategies that work, from start to finish. Take the time to learn them. There is no such thing as a natural-born salesperson. There are people with lots of confidence, but even they also need to understand the basics of selling.

THE BIGGEST REASON YOU MUST BE YOUR OWN SALESPERSON

It's called "learning the business." You can't just sit in your office, all comfortable, and avoid dealing with the outside world. At least not if you expect to succeed.

You must deal with your prospects and customers, one on one, to really understand how your business affects others. It is only by seeing your business as your potential customers see it that you can grow.

By making sales calls and having sales interviews with potential customers you'll be able to see areas where your business is strong. You'll also see areas where your business is weak. Most importantly, you may see areas of potential growth or perhaps potential problems you never thought about.

Most of my best new marketing ideas came after sales interviews with prospects and customers. It is imperative to your success that you be in touch with your customers on a regular basis. If something is wrong, you, as the owner of the business, should be the very first to know. Only you have the power to correct matters. You'll also find out who your real competition is. You'll find out what they do to make a sale, what they charge, and a whole lot more. When I was making sales calls I'd always ask a lot of questions when the prospect mentioned they had interviewed one of my competitors.

When you ask about what a competitor said or did, a few people will get very secretive, as if they had taken some kind of oath never to reveal such confidential information. I never really understood why. Perhaps they think you'll give a better deal if they withhold the information. Maybe they feel important playing such a silly game. It doesn't really matter. Never let a few duds discourage you from asking. The benefits when they do tell are fantastic.

I found many people more than willing to tell me what a competitor had said or offered. Many times they'd give me copies of literature and bid proposals left behind. You can really learn a great deal in a hurry this way.

Finally, how can anyone really expect to hire, train, and supervise salespeople if he or she can't do the job effectively? Understanding the function is one thing; doing it is another.

Supervising salespeople effectively to get results is an art in itself. It is not realistic to think you can do as well when you don't have the experience.

GETTING STARTED

This book is written in the order of a sale. I suggest you first read the entire book so you have a complete understanding of the sales process, from start to finish.

Second, go to the prospecting chapters (Chapters 3, 4, and 5) and start with the first part, which is to identify as many prospect groups as you can. Even if you have already done this before, I'd like you to do it over again. As you go down the list of questions to ask yourself I think you'll find many additional potential prospect groups.

After you've exhausted the list, rate the prospect groups on a scale of one to five. One meaning they are a long shot, but still worth an effort; five meaning they represent the easiest and most likely group of prospects available to you. Start with your best prospects, the fives.

Learning the Material

Much of what you read here will be new to you. At first it will feel a little awkward. That's to be expected. You may stumble here and there and make a few mistakes. So what? The world won't come to an end. Usually your prospects will never know the difference, and if they do, what's the worst that can happen? They won't buy from you? So what. Are they going to be the only prospect who says no?

Be willing to learn. When you learn anything new, you're bound to make a few errors—it's okay. Once you start using these various strategies you'll be amazed how people respond, how much further you'll get on every sales call, and how exciting the first order you write will be.

In Chapter 2, I discuss the One-call Sales Close concept. Remember that when you go on a sales call, your job is to focus on closing the deal, not sit around giving people a bunch of free information and advice. Amateur salespeople confuse telling people everything they know about their product or service with selling.

Remember, despite how really clever you think you are to get an appointment, the only reason the prospect allowed you into his or her home or business is that he or she is hoping in some way you can resolve a problem. Most prospects won't tell you the real scoop without your probing questions.

From the first moment you introduce yourself, you'll be asking questions and finding out why the prospect is seeing you, what problem he or she hopes you can offer a practical solution to. When you finally give information, you'll confine yourself to the issues the prospect has expressed concerns over. Forget all the good stuff you know and restrict yourself to helping your prospect resolve this problem with your product or service, then ask for the order!

Does this sound very simple? It is. Selling isn't brain surgery. What makes it complicated are salespeople who don't have a focused sales plan to sell from—people just making sales calls at random and talking about anything that comes up in conversations with prospects.

I'm going to share with you strategies, techniques, and innovative ideas for making more money than you ever dreamed possible, all through selling. There is nothing in this book that isn't simply common-sense ways to handle various selling situations. These proven strategies have made a ton of money for many salespeople for many years.

Please, join the club.

What One-call Sales Closing Means to Your Bank Account

THE "ONE-CALL CLOSE"

From here on, I'm going to work with you just like I've worked with any other sales recruit over the years. I'm going to share with you the money-making strategies that can turn your business around, the ideas and techniques I've seen work time after time.

Oh yes, one more thing. Don't think of yourself as a business owner. I want you to think like a salesperson. Every time you speak to a customer or prospect, you are a salesperson. You have one key thought to consider every time: What and how can I sell this person?

In the vast majority of all selling, in theory, people making sales calls can make a complete sale in one visit. In the vast majority of all selling, in real life, they don't. After you have read this book and applied its principles, you'll see how easy it is to close sales on one call, just about every time.

In a smaller percentage of some business situations, a person making a sales call, because of the technical or more complicated nature of what he or she sells, must visit a prospect more than one time before a final sale can be completed.

Even then you can make a mini-sale on each subsequent visit so you'll know exactly where you are in the selling process and what's needed to finish the job. No more blind alleys, no more wasted effort with less-than-honest buyers.

Finally, some sales calls are on the very same individuals, time after time, usually in situations where products are replaced or restocked on a regular basis or supplies are ordered from time to time. This is often called "route selling." In order to be profitable, sales must be made. This book will teach you the strategies of asking questions, evaluating how much potential (and thus how much time you spend) the account holds, and how to prospect for additional accounts for your route.

Some people who sell routes fall into the trap of becoming pals with the customers. They wind up trading war stories and being order takers. Truthfully, that is not selling in the real sense. I have nothing against being friendly with customers, but not to the point that you abandon your sales training. Your job is to sell. Forget all the B. S. about building company goodwill. That's just one of many excuses some people use to justify not doing their job. These are the same people who complain about low pay.

In America today, some of the highest-paid people are in sales. Many highly paid executives and business owners are proud to tell how they started their careers as a salesperson. The opportunity to earn an excellent living in selling has never been better.

So why do some people making sales calls still struggle? Because they either don't know how to sell properly or they know but don't apply the selling strategies that can make them rich. After you read and really digest the contents of this book, I promise you, you'll know how to sell!

And what if, after that, you still have difficulty in applying the good selling principles needed to make you successful? Don't despair, there's an answer and it's in this book, where I discuss self-esteem issues. Please read it carefully. It can easily change your life for the better.

Does all this sound like work? You bet it is. There are no free lunches. I have yet to meet any successful man or woman small business owner who has not admitted what a struggle success can be. At times when you feel a little down just remember that's part of life. Persistence and determination can and will succeed like nothing else. Stick with it. Stay the course. Success can and will be yours.

WHY A "ONE-CALL CLOSE"?

I spent a good chunk of my career in the burglar and fire alarm industry, part of the time selling the residential market, a much bigger part of it selling to commercial and industrial accounts.

Frequently, in my early years, I spent lots of time chasing around gathering information, walking through people's homes or business facilities doing extensive, time-consuming planning, writing detailed proposals, then making a trip to drop off the proposal, and, finally, waiting by the phone for a go-ahead call.

Most of the time, they never called. I'd call them after a period of time and usually they would be too busy to take my call. The secretary would tell me they were still considering my proposal and would call me when a decision was made.

More time passed and I'd call again, with just about the same response. About the third or fourth time I'd call they would tell me they had decided on a competitor's system, thanks anyway, goodbye.

Being a good salesperson I'd want to know where I'd failed so at least I didn't keep making the same mistake. I'd ask, "Whose system did you finally decide upon, Mr. Prospect?" or "What made you select their system over ours?"

The answer would be sharp, even nasty. "That's confidential," or "I can't give out that information," or "That's none of your business," or "Look, you just didn't measure up. I'm busy!" and they'd slam the phone, right in my ear.

It hurt to be treated like that. When I went to see them originally, they were nice, they treated me with respect. They let me spend hours designing a detailed plan to protect their premises, explaining all the options we offered, answering question after question for them, even going back to the office to research answers when necessary, then making a special trip to give them the complete proposal. What was even worse was that many of them said they were in a hurry so I'd drag the stuff home and work at my kitchen table to meet whatever deadline they had asked for.

Sometimes, after two or three big proposals blew up in my face, one right after the other, I'd get depressed. My self-esteem would take a deep plunge. I wondered if I belonged in sales. I wondered what was wrong with me, what was wrong with my company. There were times in those early years I seriously considered another career.

Then I'd close a deal, feel a little better, and continue on. I was making a living, selling my quota most of the time, but I could never break out of that rut of just making it. This went on for a few years.

Something inside me told me I was better than this, I deserved a bigger paycheck. I deserved better treatment from prospects for whom I was breaking my back. I got a little angry. I started to buy books on selling. They helped a little, but two out of three would be some guy's theory I really couldn't relate to. I took sales training courses, which were about the same. I kept at it, however, because each book or training course would offer *something* I could relate to, something I could use effectively. I was still struggling, but not quite as hard.

At that time I was single and dating. My girlfriend in those days was a college student who was going to be a social worker. One night she had to attend a group therapy session on assertiveness as part of her studies. Her car was being repaired so I drove her and took a seat in the far back of the room. I was planning to catnap while she sat up front, taking her notes. I never did.

At the meeting various people took turns describing personal situations where they were being taken advantage of in some way by a spouse, friends, kids, and so on. Most were blaming other people for their difficulties. Other people in the group, not personally involved and thus more objective, would gently suggest that the complainers were at fault for not standing up for themselves, that they actually invited, or at least allowed, the poor treatment. I was fascinated.

At the same time I became uneasy as the meeting progressed because I could see that what was happening to me as a salesperson was very similar to what these people were describing.

Did you ever have a problem in your life you were having difficulty getting a grasp on, then suddenly a light goes on, and things become clear? It happened to me that night. I could see where my behavior had something to do with the way prospects were treating me. I could see cases where I didn't make a sale because I actually would freeze up when it came time to ask for the order and I would just go on talking.

It would be easy and very impressive for me to claim that I studied assertiveness and became a dynamite salesperson over night. But life doesn't work that way. In truth, it took me a period of time to evolve, to make changes in my behavior, to be more assertive, yet never become aggressive or abusive.

I also spent time and energy studying some areas of human psychology, which I felt might apply to selling, and sales. This book contains ideas that proved out over the years, strategies that worked time after time.

If you are new to selling or if you are experienced in selling but not satisfied with your sales results, take heart. There are ways to improve yourself. There are techniques that will help. There are ways to present whatever you sell in a manner that will make people eager to buy. There are ways to determine how sincere a prospect is before you waste a lot of time. There are ways to know if you have a reasonable chance to sell a prospect.

Many people want results without working. If you are one of those, please, don't read this book. I'm going to show you more dynamite selling strategies than you have ever seen in one book, but each and every one only works if you use it, if you take the time to memorize and practice it on each sales call. There are so many strategies you can't use them all at one time. You'll need to master them one or two at a time. To be a true master salesperson takes both time and a dedication. You must want to improve yourself.

Understand, these strategies will not work every time. Nothing does except in your daydreams. In real life, expect to make mistakes, and prepare not to worry if you do. Keep practicing. Slowly but surely you will feel a new power, a new freedom you've never felt before as you genuinely master the art of selling. Nothing will surpass the confidence you feel as you make your sales calls, truly in control of your own destiny.

There is a world of selling out there that is actually fun. Why do I say "fun"? Because, when I go out selling and come back with business that means profits in my bank account; that really is my idea of a good time. I think after you finish this book, it will be yours also!

3

Finding Eager Buyers

WHO IS REALLY A PROSPECT?

Part of my time is spent as a sales and small business consultant. Often, people will come to me with new business ideas for advice. Sometimes they want to know if they should invest in someone's business venture, or in a business of their own. At some point in the conversation I'll ask "Who's going to buy this?" What I'm hoping to hear is what segment of the market do they project as viable prospects.

What often happens is their eyes open wide with genuine excitement and say "Why everybody! Everybody is a prospect!" I really cringe when people say that. Their response tells me they are in love with the idea. As most of us have learned in life, when you love something or someone, you view everything through rose-colored glasses. I know they go to sleep at night with visions of huge numbers of people flocking to this business idea, of big profits without much effort. In short, they've discovered Utopia!

It's really very common. People want to believe what other people say. We want to trust, especially if the source is a relative or acquaintance. We all tend to do it. I'll admit to doing it more than once in my business career. I'll also tell you that each time I did, the rose-colored glasses got knocked off and I wound up a loser in one way or another.

Put two people in a room and I promise, you'll have a disagreement over something. Everybody is different from everybody else in some fashion. Therefore, not everybody is a prospect for anything.

19

Yet it's this very diversity that gives salespeople so much opportunity. Because people are so different, almost any business can find someone eager (yes, I said eager) to buy their services or products. But to be effective, you must know how to prospect.

Prospecting is simply finding out who is and who is not a potential customer for your business. In order for your business to succeed, you must have a reliable method of finding new customers. You should also know what a buyer looks like. Finally, when you do find that person, you ought to know how to qualify them. Here is how to proceed.

Analyze Your Ideal Buyer

In this step you may come up with several different profiles, which is not unusual. A lot of products and services are purchased by different groups of people. Actually, the more types of buyers you come up with, the better. For instance, if your business is selling copy machines, the best prospects are those who have large volumes of paperwork.

Breaking this down further, insurance companies, law firms, and accounting firms are three (of many) prospect subgroups that would tend to make lots of copies. There is no research source that will list large users of paper. However, you can easily locate insurance, legal, and accounting firms. Also, reference materials will show the size of these firms so you can start with the largest (best prospects) first.

Perhaps you sell a service, working from your home. Let's say you have a computer and laser printer and do desktop publishing, such as advertisements and brochures. Who needs you?

In this case, since computers and laser printers are common in larger firms, your best shot is smaller firms who don't own them. Your second best shot is the larger firms who are overworked and need someone to handle the overflow. Printers, advertising agencies, public-relations firms, and graphics firms are additional prospects. While they may own computers they often work under tight deadlines and may need a reliable resource to complete work on a timely basis. For them, especially the small ones with limited staff, it's often less costly to farm out certain jobs.

Common Customer Denominators

Before you can sell anything, you must first identify who your best prospects are. The better job you do at this stage, the more successful your sales efforts will be. This information will tell you many things, such as how to find prospects, what sales appeals to use, and how many prospects may be out there. It is not uncommon to come up with several different profiles since many products or services have broad appeal. In that case, work them one at a time, selecting your best first. This is a generic list, with questions for both business and individual prospects. Feel free to add to it as needed. If you have your own business, the library, past customers, and studying competitors are common resources. If you are a dealer, check with the manufacturer, who may have already prepared a profile. If you are a salesperson, chances are your company has already done so.

What do my customers look like? What common traits exist so I can find them easily?

Business firms, kinds _____

Company size _____ SICs _____

Job title of likely buyer _____

Business association memberships _____

Trade association memberships _____

Geography _____

Business publications read _____

Trade publications read _____

Individuals, age groups _____

Mostly married/single/widowed/divorced __ Mostly male or female __

Shopping/buying habits _____

Club memberships _____

Publications read _____

TV/Radio favorites _____

Hobbies _____

Where and how do my *successful* competitors find them _____

Common customer denominators.

There are several ways to prospect these potential customers. The easy way is to obtain a directory, perhaps a phone-book listing, of all printers, graphics firms, advertising agencies, and PR firms in your area. With printers, you'd want to speak to the owner or manager. Talking to ad, graphics, and PR firms, you'd want to speak to the art director. In most cases, these would be the people who make the decisions.

Prospecting for larger firms with overflow work or small companies who need desktop publishing is more difficult. The problem is, there are no directories or research materials that will identify these firms from a research standpoint.

These prospects will more likely be found by telemarketing, cold calls, or direct mail to lists of business firms. Personal observation, while somewhat limited, helps. It's simply noticing what's around you at all times from a prospecting standpoint.

For instance, our desktop publisher goes into a supermarket for the week's groceries. She notices a community bulletin board in the front entrance with signs and advertising flyers. She copies down names, addresses, and phone numbers of any advertisers who look like they could use desktop publishing, and calls later to offer her services. To further expand on this she could read local newspapers and watch for advertisers who look like they could use some design help. There are many such advertisers, especially in smaller newspapers.

Personal observation is often a way of life for good salespeople. When they meet people at a party, they find out how these contacts might possibly pertain to their business. When they do business with someone, they make it a point to tell what they do for a living, being very generous with business cards. You have to hand out a lot of cards for any to start coming back, but cards are cheap. If you get one person out of 100 to call you back and become a customer, you've come out ahead.

You can increase these odds dramatically. As you hand someone your card, ask, "Do you happen to know anyone I should be talking to about (whatever you sell)?" Sometimes people say no, think about it, and call you a few days later. Sometimes it's not the person to whom you gave the card who calls, but someone he or she told to call you. Who cares? Most times, it's a good prospect.

Researching for Prospects

The easiest way to find buyers is to locate them in some kind of listing or directory. You'd be surprised how many successful small business firms have developed entire sales strategies using the basic telephone directory as their reference.

A few pages back I told you to analyze your potential buyers and gave you a few examples of how to do this. Following is the formula to use for any product or service.

To do this effectively, prepare a profile of who your prospective customer is. As I said, if you get several different profiles, so much the better. Just understand that it's best to tackle them one at a time. You do that by looking over your list and selecting your best prospects first, then second best, and so on.

Next, try to locate a common denominator—things these prospect groups have in common and might relate to, locating them through research. For instance, if your best prospects are manufacturers of screw machine products, then there's an excellent chance a trade association exists for them. Trade associations can be found through a library search. One popular book that lists trade associations is published by Gale's; there are others also.

Trade associations can help you several ways. They may have a membership list or directory you can obtain. From that you can select firms that would be appropriate to call on, such as prospects in certain areas. If it's a national association and you only want local members, you can ask if they have a local chapter and contact them. Trade associations frequently publish newsletters that accept ads. Better yet, they sometimes publish annual industry directories, which are frequently used by people in the industry. Sometimes you can get a free listing as a vendor to their industry. I would not spend more than a token amount for ads, if that. Large amounts spent on ads are a very poor investment. The point of this exercise is to find people you can call on, not to advertise and sit back waiting for the phone to ring. It very rarely works that way.

Libraries: A Gold Mine of Information

I can't think of a better place to start your prospecting efforts than your library. When you know what prospects you are seeking, then you can begin to identify the researchable traits they may have in common. Sharing this information with your librarian who works in the research department and enlisting his or her help will usually produce results.

There are many ways to find prospect names in a library. I always make it a point to ask for the reference department. Here are a few, but your local librarian will know many more.

Chambers of Commerce. A great resource. You can locate them through your library. Nearly every community has one and often several exist near larger, more populated areas.

Street Directories. Published in many communities, these are like phone books, but they list by street address instead of name. Excellent if you want to contact everyone in a certain geographic area.

Manufacturers Directories. Looking for a company that manufacturers certain products? Or just manufacturers? There are companies that print comprehensive directories of manufacturing firms throughout the United States and even worldwide. Some publish statewide and even citywide books. They are usually broken down by geographic location and by SIC, an identifying number that indicates what business they are in. The library will have a list of the SIC Codes.

Trade Publications. Obtaining information on an industry can sometimes be done by reading trade publications. Selling to candy manufacturers? They have their own trade magazines. Selling to lingerie shops? They also have trade publications. Unfortunately, these publications are not sold at magazine stands; they are only promoted to industry insiders. Reading them can give you a wealth of information and an insight to the needs of the industry.

You can locate trade publications by industry, then, if you're interested, write to the publication for subscription rates. If you think you may wish to advertise, write on company letterhead to their advertising manager. Ask for an advertising rate card and sample copy of their publications. This usually gets a quick response.

Telephone Directories. While you may not need to visit a library for a local telephone directory, many libraries have directories from other cities and states. This is an excellent way to locate potential buyers in other areas before you visit or to develop mailing and calling lists. Also, you can call your local telephone company and request that phone books for other communities be sent to your home or office.

Checking Out the Competition

In order to sell your services or product(s), you need to know what you are up against. It pays to research your competition. The more you know about them and how they do their job, the better you'll do yours.

Like profit margins, this is an area newcomers to the business world become nervous about. They may feel it's wrong to try to find out what competitors are doing, sort of like stealing.

You won't hear successful, more experienced businesspeople talk like that. They know the value of knowing what they are up against. They also are not surprised when their competitors start checking them out. It's important for you to have some reasonable idea of what your competitors say and offer when they speak to the same people you will be trying to sell.

One point I want to make: I do not ever, ever advocate doing anything illegal to collect information on your competition. To stoop that low makes a person a common criminal, who, frankly, doesn't belong in business.

Strategies on Gathering Information about the Competition

1. Watch for their advertisements. How, when, and where they advertise gives you a clue as to whom they consider salable

prospects. I keep a clip file to see what trends develop over a period of time.

2. Ask customers and prospects what the competition said and offered when they called on them. While some people won't tell you, many will. Ask if the competitor left any literature or, better yet, price quotes, and if you can see them, perhaps copy them. Don't let a few people who may decline to provide these stop you from asking. Being familiar with what your competitors say and leave behind can be a very valuable eye-opener.

3. Visit the library. Publications and directories from your industry can be very revealing. Study your industry well.

4. Join a trade association (and become active in it) if there is one for your industry. Not only does it keep you abreast of the latest developments in your business, you'll also get to meet your competitors face to face. Often, the competitors you used to think of as jerks (or worse) will turn out to be very nice people. As long as you are not in direct competition with them, many will share money-making ideas with peers.

   A word of warning: Never forget that these people *are* your competitors in some fashion. If you start speaking carelessly about the identity of your customers, confidential deals, business problems, or anything else that may help a competitor, you may live to regret it. It's not a good idea to get overinvolved because, as you'll see in the next chapter, there are other membership situations that can pay big financial dividends.

5. Visit a competitor's location if appropriate. This applies more to retailers, but in all businesses it's good to see how competitors operate.

What's Your Niche?

Sometimes businesspeople, fearing no business at all, will take any work offered. I remember visiting a consulting client in the printing business. His office, staffed by three people besides himself, was total chaos—phones ringing, people frantically calling and trying to schedule things. It was a zoo. It also puzzled me. He had hired me to determine why his sales were so low and to show him how to sell more effectively.

"I don't see why you need me. It looks like you are up to capacity," I said.

"We are. Unfortunately this is all printing work we have to job out to larger printers. My presses don't have this capacity," he replied.

To make a long, confusing, story short, it turned out that he started taking on whatever work came through the door. He was barely making any profit on the work because he was only the middleman, not the actual printer. On top of that he had little control over delivery time or quality of work done by the other printers. Every time there was a complaint he had to refer it to the printer involved, get an answer, and call the customer back. It was a logistical nightmare. The worst part was, he was this busy and still in serious trouble paying his bills.

I told him, "At this pace, you don't even have time to work with me to develop a new sales strategy. And, if we can't do that, you don't need me. If fact, I doubt by next month you'll be able to afford me."

He asked me to be patient. Somehow he'd find time to work with me. He just couldn't let go of this work. It was all he had, he said. While I felt sorry for his predicament, I knew he was deluding himself. When I declined to work with him until he had the time, he agreed not to continue taking on work he could not print.

We worked together, developing a strategy for locating buyers for the printing he could do in his own plant at a reasonable profit. By then his three employees were idle so I showed them and the boss some easy sales-call techniques. I got all four people involved in the selling process, which did not make the secretary and the guy who ran the printing press the happiest of campers. They knew, however, that the company was in dire straits and this was a necessary plan to save everybody's job.

The first week was rocky, with little results and a depressed group. The second week, they nabbed two decent-sized jobs. By the end of the fourth week, only the owner was selling, while the other three employees were busy again, this time with work the company could afford to handle. Several months later I went back again, this time to assist in the hiring and training of a new full-time salesperson.

The point of this story is that every industry has both strong and weak points. If you have 10 competitors furnishing the identical product or service, the competition will kill you.

The smart sales angle is to know your customers very well, know your competitors very well, and carefully observe what is not being addressed in the marketplace.

Concentrate your selling efforts on areas you can serve well at a decent profit. Don't be afraid to specialize, so long as there are enough potential buyers in the marketplace.

Another strength for the small business is service. By your smaller size, you can give more personalized service to your customers than a larger competitor can. There are many customers who will pay a premium for top service. Being the low bidder isn't always the right way to go.

Common-sense Prospecting

Every business has a different set of problems, yet the very same principles discussed earlier apply to all. What may appear at first to be very different problems, because you are in a different industry, are really the same ones. This book is primarily concerned with direct selling, that is, situations where a sales call is made to solicit business. However, let me share some basics from the retailing business that directly apply. No matter what or how you sell, you can apply the principles outlined for your business. Here are a few examples. For a grocery store, people who buy food within a certain number of miles from the store are the best prospects. Since that covers a huge number of people, most groceries use newspaper ads to prospect, offering special prices, convenient hours, and so on.

Unknown to the public, a lot of newspapers print zone editions. The main pages are all the same, but certain inside sections, such as the food pages, are printed separately and distributed in specific sections of the city. For instance, a grocer on the east side of a large city can buy advertising in just that area. He knows that on the west side his ads will be pretty much ignored since most people don't want to travel long distances for food. (He knows what a prospect looks like and also knows that even for such a common item as food, not everyone is a prospect for his business). Direct mail to specific neighborhoods near the facility is also common.

Let's look at a beauty salon located next door to the grocery store. Every woman likes to look nice, right? Does that mean every woman is a prospect for that salon? No, not at all. In fact, the salon owner has to define further who is and who is not a prospect in order to survive.

How does the salon owner do this? First, the owner must make some generalizations about who might come to the salon. An obvious key is women who take pride in their appearance. There might be working women who are out in public and feel a need to look good, but may not have a lot of time, or women who go out on weekends, perhaps to dinner or a show. There are many more prospects, but these few definitions are sufficient for the purpose of this example. When you prepare such an exercise for your business, always make the list as long as you can, within reason.

Let's see what the above information can tell us. First, working women prospects will respond favorably to evening and weekend hours available at the salon. As working people, they should have some disposable income to spend on their appearance. As to how much to charge, what kind of neighborhood are we in—lower, middle, or upper income? What does the competition do? Are they failing to meet potential demands, such as special hours for working women, which we can offer (called a marketing niche).

Another prospect is women who go out on weekends, perhaps socially or to dinners, movies, and so on. The higher the income in the neighborhood the salon is located in, the more women there will be with disposable income to frequent the salon.

A note on retail pricing: Higher prices usually work best in better-income areas. Dirt-cheap prices in higher-income neighborhoods are thought of as lower quality. The higher the income of an area, the less people are concerned about cost and the more they are concerned about quality.

Conversely, a shop in a lower-income area can do well by concentrating on less-customized services and focusing on lower-cost specials, making it easier for women with limited incomes, who might otherwise not visit a salon, to become customers.

So, how does our salon owner reach these markets? It's important to take into account the habits of the people you're targeting. The working woman might respond to advertising flyers passed out where she works (the pitch is, she can come in at lunchtime or right after work, making it easy on her), an ad in business publications aimed especially at women, a newspaper zone ad directed at your neighborhood, and direct mail to selected lists.

What about the ladies who like to go out on weekends but may not work? Advertising on theater screens and programs is available in some areas. Other possibilities are running a promotion with a restaurant, coupon specials distributed in your marketing area, and the newspaper zone ad.

As you read this, I hope one thing becomes clear to you: the value of understanding your prospective customers. If you can think in the terms they do, if you can think about what they might expect from a business like yours, if you will "walk a mile in their moccasins," you'll be selling from a position of strength. You'll sell more because you'll be helping people get what they want, not what you think they should have. You'll keep your customers longer because you'll be one of the few salespeople they will ever meet who really cares about addressing their needs.

I'm big on mottoes and sayings. When I run a training seminar on prospecting, I give all the attendees a motto that sums up this entire chapter:

"People don't buy for your reasons,
they buy for theirs."

4

Big-Money Prospecting Strategies

Now we get down to the bread-and-butter techniques of finding good prospects. Notice I used the word "good"? A good prospect is one who meets certain qualifications. As you learn the methods in this chapter, you'll see that what we start out with are suspects, not prospects.

What's the difference? A suspect is someone whom you have a logical reason to believe *may* need what you sell. A prospect is a suspect you have further qualified as to ability and interest in buying what you sell.

The world is filled with suspects for just about any product or service you may sell. When you are locating and working with suspects, you don't want to spend large amounts of time with any one suspect. If you have difficulty determining if they are or are not prospects, then I suggest passing them by and going to the next one.

This is another area beginning salespeople frequently have problems with. They spend too much time working with suspects. Unless you happen to be in a line of business that really has a very limited number of suspects, which is rare, then at this stage of compiling lists of suspects, keep time involvement to a minimum. For instance let's say I have a list of 200 suspects, 190 are local and 10 of them are out of town. At this point I have no way of knowing who is and who is not going to buy. I have a lot of work ahead of me because I have to qualify everybody on this list.

The 10 out-of-town suspects will require a long-distance call (or two) to reach, while the 190 locals can be reached with a local call. If the out-of-towners are not in when I call, it's an additional expense to call again. If they turn into prospects then I have ahead of me a long trip to see them. In the same amount of time it takes to visit 10 out-of-towners I could call on 20 or 30 local suspects. In this particular case, it does not pay for me to get involved trying to chase 10 distant suspects. I would either throw them away or give them to a noncompetitive associate who might have an easier time getting to them.

In your business it will be important to determine the limits to which you will chase a suspect. The more easy-to-reach suspects you have, the less you want to chase the tough ones. Of course the reverse is also true. If you have a limited number of people to call on, then you must extend yourself much further. It simply becomes a matter of good time management. Use your time well.

THE GOLD-MINER ANALOGY

In the last century, gold miners flocked to the western part of the United States in search for gold, which in the 1800s was mined by hand. They would locate a claim, frequently along running water from a higher mountain area. With a shovel they'd dig out dirt, placing it in a shallow pan. Under the running water from the stream they would carefully shake and twist the pan so the earth would separate and slowly empty into the stream. As the dirt separated, any nuggets or flecks of gold hidden in the dirt would be revealed.

If this sounds like a lot of work, it was. For a few precious ounces of gold they had to handle literally tons of dirt. So why do it? Because they knew if they were persistent, the opportunity to become wealthy was very real. But what about all the stories of gold miners who went bust and never found anything but bruised knuckles and aching backs? In some cases they were simply the victims of poor luck in choosing a place to prospect.

But, some of them lost out because they simply *gave up too soon.* It's that old rule that 20 percent of the people will account for 80 percent of the successes in just about anything in life. Sure, it sounded exciting to be a rich gold miner, but the minute the work got difficult, the minute they experienced failure, people started to drop out.

There are all kinds of stories in the western part of the United States telling of new prospectors who took over a so-called worthless claim that had been worked and abandoned by others, and became millionaires. The difference between one person being a failure and another becoming a millionaire, all on the same identical claim, was persistence.

In the business world and especially in selling, just as with everything else in life, you have choices. You can be an 80-percent person or a 20-percent person. I can spend my whole life teaching how the 20 percent become very successful in selling, but most of the people I teach will not really apply the principles. Oh sure, they'll have reasons. I call them face-saving excuses for avoiding hard work. You face that choice now. You can read this book all day and night, over and over. You can plan and scheme endlessly. However, unless you go out and actually start applying these principles, nothing good happens. The old adage, "Actions speak louder than words" is valid. Be a 20-percent person!

Everything we do in this chapter will get us suspects, and lots of them. In Chapter 5, I'll show you how we get excellent prospects out of these lists of suspects, many of them actually happy to hear (and buy) from you.

For now, let's go "suspecting." Below is a comprehensive list of prospecting success methods that are time tested. These are all proven techniques, used by some of the world's most successful (and richest) businesspeople. There are by far more ways listed here than you can effectively pursue at any one time. My suggestion is that you read the entire list, then go back and select a few of the tactics that make the most sense in your situation. Keep in mind that most of the suspects you uncover ultimately will not be buyers of your product or service. At this stage of the sales plan that's to be expected. What you are doing here is simply "panning tons of dirt for those few gold nuggets" as the miners did.

If it gets a little discouraging, just remember that there are eager buyers (gold nuggets) out there in all that dirt who will be happy to see and buy from you.

One problem I have with many people in today's workforce is an avoidance of anything that appears difficult. When I work with new salespeople in training classes I often hear comments (with a little whining thrown in) such as, "There should be an easy way to do this." In my personal experiences in life, as with many other successful people I've discussed this with, we all agree that nothing worthwhile obtaining is really easy.

Certainly some people get lucky and once in a while great opportunities literally fall into their hands. Unfortunately, this is so rare in life that those who feel this is how life should be wind up bitterly disappointed. If success were that easy, everybody would be a success. However, what's really exciting in our society is that everybody has a chance for some degree of success.

Another thing to remember is that as you wade through all those names of suspects you are also handling the names of eager, interested buyers. It's your job as a salesperson for your business to find them. Let's get started.

Success Method 1: Telemarketing

This is really an excellent way for a salesperson to prospect. In some cases you will actually sell by phone. In most cases, however, it's best used to introduce yourself and obtain an appointment. Telemarketing is so important to your success, that I've devoted three chapters to it. However, please don't jump ahead, but continue to read on so you can better evaluate your options in an orderly fashion.

Success Method 2: Business Cards

I have learned to consider business cards a big waste of money and a detriment to selling when making sales calls. The one exception is when prospecting. Then I always carry them with me.

Why are they a waste when you are face to face with a prospect in an actual selling situation? Because prospects, stalling about making a decision, will fall back on "Do you have a business card?" If you are foolish enough to offer one they next say "Great, we'll get in touch." If you believe that lie, I have a great bridge in Brooklyn, New York, for sale.

When people I'm in the sales process with ask for a business card my answer is simply, "No, I don't have one." I look right at them, but say nothing more. It throws them off the stall tactic. Some even wait for me to explain further. I don't. I just continue to look at them as if they are going to continue speaking.

After a brief, uncomfortable moment they suddenly grab a pen and say "Well, let me have your phone number so I can get in touch with you." My answer is, "Why?" This again throws people. They don't expect the response. Their experience with salespeople is usually with ones who grovel for business—the 80-percent people. I'm not a grovel person. I'm a 20-percent person. So next they'll say, perhaps a little befuddled or even slightly annoyed, "So I can let you know our decision if we're going to buy from you."

"Oh," I say, "you were planning to buy something?"

"I'm not sure, we have to think it over," comes the reply.

With a puzzled look I ask, "Think it over . . ." My voice trails off.

"Yes, we need to . . ." The prospects usually will start explaining *what* they have to think over, which is why I do this behavior in the first place.

If they don't volunteer a reason I continue with a puzzled question. "Tell me, we covered so much, I'm a little confused. Just what part of this do you want to think over?"

What happens when you are asked for a business card after a sales presentation is called a "stall." For reasons unknown to you, the prospect has decided not to buy and now wants to get rid of you as quickly as possible. I really don't carry cards with me on sales presentations. The minute I hand one over, I'm finished.

Conversely, if I play out this little word game, I have an opportunity to find out just why a stall is happening. Once you can identify the reason for the stall, then you can respond appropriately.

I'll continue this discussion in later chapters that deal with the selling process. Here, this example illustrates my attitude that in most kinds of selling you need a valid decision to buy or not to buy now or a very valid reason to ever talk to that person again. "Thinking it over" is never a valid reason. If you go to someone's place to sell them, leave your business cards in the car or at the office.

So When Are Business Cards of Value?

At all stages of prospecting. If you go out for a social or business evening event, you never know who you may meet that may turn into a customer or refer you to someone who might become a customer. Any place you go at any time where you meet anybody is a time to have a clean business card ready to hand out.

Another technique I've used effectively is to have Rolodex cards printed like business cards. You'd be surprised at how many people depend on Rolodex card files for record keeping of clients and vendors. One type of Rolodex card has a little tab at the top where you can have a printer print a name or keyword pertaining to your business, such as "Insurance," "Real Estate," "Photographer," and so on. A great many companies frequently have Rolodex files, often kept on a key secretary's desk. When the boss starts yelling he or she needs something, it's usually the first place the secretary looks.

Success Method 3: Chambers of Commerce

Most chambers are business activity centers. Their sole purpose is to help members do business. Unfortunately some are very dormant organizations and a big waste of time. If you have a local one I'd suggest calling them for information and membership details. While on the phone get a couple of names of current members. Check out the chamber by first studying their literature. Do they have networking events? Business shows? Luncheons with interesting speakers? A strong membership among the business community? Next, phone (or better yet, go meet personally) the people who are already members. Ask them if the chamber provides a positive business environment for meeting prospective clients for your business. Be truthful and tell them you're looking for membership in an organization that will help you find new business. Don't pretend to be above all that and say you just want to join because you are civic minded. You won't get the answers you need to make a valid decision. Keep in mind you will be spending your hard-earned money for membership. You have every right to benefit by doing so.

Success Method 4: Business and Trade Associations Attended by Your Best Prospects

A favorite of mine. First, I believe you should have business contacts within your own industry. That usually means joining an association in your industry. I do not, however, advocate spending a lot of time and effort in any association where you can't get new business.

I know, I know. I can hear people howling now about how selfish I am to suggest that. Perhaps I am. As a businessperson you will have only a limited number of hours to do anything, and that includes selling. If you have a family to support, a mortgage to pay, creditors, and so on, as most of us do, then your obligations are deep. My feeling is our first responsibility is to those who love us and depend on us for financial support. To me, that means I spend every hour as productively as possible.

If you are going to spend valuable time at a business luncheon, a trade association, or club meeting, volunteering for a committee and so on, why not do it in front of potential new customers? If you are going to shine and be a great guy or gal in some organization, why not let yourself be admired by people who can perhaps do some business with you. There's an old saying I believe to be true, "People like to do business with people they know."

Membership alone won't do much. There are two critical keys to success here. One is to join only if you can attend the meetings regularly. Second is, get involved. Over the years I've discovered in most organizations that nearly all the members simply show up for the meetings and events. Only a very small number ever give any effort by helping to run it. If you join, be sure to watch for an opportunity to volunteer for something. They won't expect a lot out of any one person, but whatever you promise to do, do it and do it well.

Never agree to do something you may not be able to do. Your purpose here is to set a great example in front of people who may buy from you. Set a bad example and you'll be considered a jerk by those same people. Everybody in a business organization under-stands if you simply beg off with "Gee, I'd love to but I'm afraid I won't have enough time to do the task properly." However, once you make the commitment to something you can do, set aside a few hours a week and focus on doing it well.

I promise you that over a reasonably short period of time you'll be well known and involved in the group. People will see you as a person with credibility and integrity. They will see you as someone who gets things done, a winner, and will admire you for it. If you have done this in an organization of potential customers, business opportunities will come to you that you'd never find otherwise in a million years. If you do it in an organization of your competitors, plan to settle for a handshake.

Success Method 5: Personal Observation

To me this is such an obvious way to make money that I almost did not include it here because I had mentioned it before. I'm including it to give a little nudge to those of you out there who may be passing up what I used to call free money. Here's an example of how I used personal observation when I was in the security alarm business.

Driving down a street, I would observe any empty retail stores or commercial buildings with for-rent signs. I'd watch businesses for signs of break-ins (broken plate glass, covered by a plywood board is an obvious one). I always had a notepad and attached pen on the car seat next to me. If I had no time to stop, I'd scribble down the addresses for a follow-up visit.

I'd call on the establishment that had been broken into and simply give them my card, using the technique I'll teach you later in the book. A percentage would want me to quote right on the spot. For the empty building I had stickers printed that in part said, "For connection of alarm system call..." I would paste a sticker on the front window glass. When people move into a new facility they frequently don't know who to call for an alarm system. Instead of hoping they would pick me out of 50 advertisers in the phone book, I made it easy to have them call me. Many did. Many purchased from me, never even bothering to call anyone else. I was easy to find at a time when they had lots going on.

What personal observation boils down to is simply thinking about what your most logical prospects look like, then taking action when you see one. For example, I have friends in the insurance business and others in the investment business. They always read business publications and business sections of the newspapers. They send cards of congratulations out to those listed as being promoted, and so on, following up with a phone call. Why? Simply because my sales friends know these people are at a stage in life where they may have an increased income and be thinking of investments or insurance as a protection for their future.

You need to give some serious thought to how personal observation can be of help to you. The best way is to have a good idea of what your best prospects look like. How might you run across them? When you read a newspaper, business magazine, and so on, how might you identify a good prospect? Driving down a street, in your business, would personal observation be of help? How? Where do your best prospects hang out? A luncheon club? An association or trade organization? Chamber of Commerce? Social group?

Success Method 6: Tips Clubs, Networking Groups

When I was young they used to be called tips clubs. Today the in term is networking groups. Whatever you call them, the ones that will be of big help to you will actually focus on the exchange of names of prospects among business- and salespeople. I say that because if you get in the wrong organization you can burn a lot of time (and money in some cases) with little or no results.

There are a few organizations I would avoid if my purpose was to obtain business. First, any group called a support group is usually there to provide encouragement as its primary goal. Most people there are not prospects nor are they there to help you find prospects. They are, in general, needy people looking for confirmation in some way from others that they are okay. Believe me, I'm not knocking them. I think these groups serve a valid purpose. This, however, is a chapter on how to get business so you can pay your bills, and support groups are not a good place for that.

The other organization I'd avoid as a prospecting source is any trade association of my own industry. No question that you can have a lot of fun there and meet nice people, but, again, these people are not there to give you business.

On a positive note there are also events now billed as networking events, which are sometimes sponsored by a business publication or Chamber of Commerce. They are usually held in the middle of the week, have a cash bar, booths sponsored by companies who sell to other businesspeople, and charge a small admission fee. You can sometimes meet people at these events who may buy from you. I usually go to them when they occur and I'd suggest you do the same.

Whether you get any business depends on how many people you talk to (and give out business cards to) and just plain luck. Just attending however is a real waste of your time. I've seen people go to these events, have a drink, walk around the exhibits, and then leave, complaining about what a waste of time it was. Even worse, some will go with a friend and spend the entire time talking to that person. You need to meet and talk to people, lots and lots of people, during the event to be productive.

Working a Meeting of Strangers

Here's how to work effectively a networking meeting of strangers. Buy a professionally made name badge with your first and last name and business name printed below it. Pin it on your right lapel, so when you extend your hand to shake it's easy for someone to see. Take a supply of business cards, counted out, say 20 to start. Promise yourself you won't leave until you have given the whole stack out.

When you walk in the door, smile and never stop until you have left the meeting. If you come with a friend, separate until the event ends. Go out of your way to make eye contact with people. Most will be shy and look away. The minute you get a return look, walk to the person, smiling, extend your hand to shake theirs and simply say "Hi, my name's———, I sell (benefit), you are?" Let them answer. Never say what you are such as, "I'm in real estate." Say, rather, what it means as a benefit to a buyer such as, "I'm in the business of finding people their ideal home."

I've gone to some networking meetings with no results and attended some where I found excellent customers, people I would probably never have the opportunity to meet elsewhere. Often I'll meet other salespeople doing what I'm doing, prospecting. If they are in an allied but noncompetitive field to me they often turn into sources of great sales leads. I of course share with them as well.

The idea at these events is to meet a lot of different potential prospects, get their business cards, and then follow up. I never spend more than 5 or 10 minutes with any one person. If this person sounds like a possibility, I ask for his or her card, give mine in return, and promise to follow up with a call. I write immediately a few notes on the card so I won't forget later why I'm calling.

Tips/Leads Exchange Clubs

What will make you big bucks is a group of other salespeople and small businesspeople who are actively making sales calls on a regular basis, who do not conflict with you by selling the same or similar products or services you do, and whose sole purpose in meeting is to trade names of potential prospects. These are the groups I would go out of my way to find. This is where you can spend your time somewhat productively.

There are some people who have started businesses doing this. These are organizations where you pay a membership fee to join and often a weekly meeting fee as well. In my area of the country there are two I know of, each with 15 to 20 local groups meeting weekly. Because the organizers of these groups charge a fee, it becomes an issue if you don't get enough prospects to at least pay the cost of membership.

Before I'd pay anyone to join, I'd ask for an opportunity to attend at least one if not two meetings as a sample and just pay for any food (they are almost always breakfast meetings). At the meeting I'd find out what the various members do for a living and evaluate if they are the kind of people whose daily routine would put them in contact with prospects for what I sell. Watch the atmosphere and behavior. Are these successful people or a bunch of losers? Are they just looking out for themselves or is there really an atmosphere of sharing? Are most attendees negative or positive? Never forget: Losers hang out with losers, winners with winners. Go where the success is or don't go.

In its true form, tips clubs or leads clubs among sales and small businesspeople are informal, with little or no fees charged. They usually make a deal with a conveniently located restaurant to save a space for the group for a weekly early breakfast meeting, everyone paying for his or her own food. While I'm positive they exist in most areas, sometimes locating them can require some detective work, since they have no phone book listing or place of business. To find them, ask other salespeople and/or call the editors of the local business magazines or newspapers. Also, check the business calendar listings that many business magazines and newspapers print.

It's relatively easy to start your own club. Just start speaking to other salespeople. You'll meet lots of them at the networking events I discussed above.

Here are a few simple rules to attract successful salespeople and businesspeople to join (the only kind you should have).

1. Meet early in the morning so you don't cut into people's selling time. The more successful the salesperson, the more preoccupied he or she is with not wasting valuable selling time.

2. Have a firm time to start and also to end each meeting.

3. Structure the meeting so everybody has a chance to speak for a few minutes, describing what they sell and, more importantly, what kind of prospects they are seeking. Put specific limits on how long someone can talk. Never allow anyone to dominate a meeting or you'll lose members.

4. Keep the meeting focused on its purpose, and keep it in a positive tone. Don't allow it to become a general bull or gripe session.

5. Limit membership to one person from each line of products or services.

Success Method 7: The Telephone Book

Before you pass this up for a more exotic prospect list, let me tell you the telephone book is always the very first place I consider. Everyone in your area with a published telephone is right there, in your hands. On top of that it's free and immediately accessible.

Most salespeople who use the phone book get discouraged because they don't understand how to prospect effectively. If you sell to business firms then use the business listings to find appropriate suspects. If you sell to individuals, use the home phone listing. I would not start in the A's when contacting suspects in the home phone listing. Too many people do that. The A's and other people in the front of the book get a lot of calls and mail; the people in the middle and end very few. I always go to the middle of the alphabet or go backwards from the Z's. Salespeople who know how to prospect effectively start getting business from additional sources such as referrals and no longer rely on the phone book as a total means of prospecting.

Success Method 8: Ask Everybody the Magic Words

I told you earlier to learn as much as you can about your prospects and develop a few words to describe them to others. When I was in the security business I was always alert to people just moving into a business or home and people who had just experienced a break-in. I considered them good suspects. It became such a habit that after a while I never realized I was doing it. I'd never ask "Who do you know who wants a security system?" They always say no one. However, it all changed quickly when I'd ask, "Who do you know who recently moved?" or "Who do you know who recently had a break-in?"

I recently trained salespeople who sell car phones. Salespeople and people on the go are two of their best prospects. I trained the salespeople to ask, "How many friends of yours are in sales?" and "Tell me who this describes: a friend of yours who is always on the go and never at home when you call?"

Think of your best prospects. Develop questions you can ask that best describe the traits you need for a good prospect.

Success Method 9: The Address Book

Sometimes it doesn't matter if you sell people or not. If you end up at their home or office to make a presentation, always use this technique. If they buy from you they feel pretty good at that moment and won't mind supplying what you ask for. If they *didn't* buy from you, giving you what you ask for becomes an easy way for them to feel less guilty.

First, use the questions I just explained in Success Method 8, which get you thinking in terms of what you need. Next ask, "Mary, where do you keep telephone numbers for reference?" After she replies say, "Could you get them please?" (Don't make the mistake of asking for their phone book. People often keep no phone book but lots of little scraps of paper in bags, desk drawers, on refrigerators, and so on.) Ask the prospect to go through them for each prospect question. While this doesn't work every time, most people will do it for you with a little encouragement.

At this point, most salespeople stop here, take the names, and contact them later. Not me: I always used to go just a little bit further. Here is how a typical conversation might go:

Me: "Well Bill, it looks like this isn't for you, do we agree on that?"

Prospect: "Yes, I think you're right. It's a shame you had to drive all that way."

Me: "Thanks Bill. I appreciate your concern. Perhaps you might do me a small favor."

Prospect: "I'll try, what is it?"

Me: "Bill, put yourself in my shoes for just a minute. Who do you have in your address book who ... "

When the prospect comes up with some names, I'll say:

Me: "Bill, of all those names, who would it make the most sense to call on first?"

Prospect: (Gives me a name)

Me: "Do you have his phone number?"

Prospect: "Yes."

Me: "Could you please dial his number and tell him I'll be over shortly?"

Now if you think people won't call a friend and make an appointment for your sales call, you're half right. Do this properly and half won't. But half will. I've gotten introduced to people this way who were next to unapproachable any other way and I've made some pretty big sales I would have never gotten otherwise.

What about the half who won't call for you? My answer is, Who cares? Most of the time they feel embarrassed to say no to you. The ones who think you are a little pushy will just say something about "you should be doing that."

Success Method 10: Cold Calls

This is the real biggie among salespeople because this is the one kind of prospecting most people will find all kinds of excuses not to do. Notice that I stuck it at the back end of the prospecting techniques? I did that on purpose. I wanted you to see that there are always other choices in addition to cold calls. If I made it Success Method 1, which it really is, some people would not read any further. Cold calls can be a scary business.

Entire books have been written about cold-calling tactics and strategies. I know plenty of different ways of cold calling, but in this book I'm only going to tell you one. It's the easiest and least stressful I know of. It also works better than anything else I've ever tried.

I call it the "I was just at your neighbor's" technique. Here's how it goes:

"Good morning, my name is Jones, Bill Jones. I'm with (*your business name*). I was just working with one of your neighbors. He (she) had a problem with (*here you state the problem, no sales stuff, just the problem as a prospect might see it*). I was able to help solve (*simply restate problem, and don't stick in any sales stuff*). Since I'm in the area, I thought I'd check with you folks to see if (*problem again, perhaps a second problem you can solve*) might be a concern. We've been very successful at helping people in these situations."

Why is this easier and less stressful on the salesperson? Because you don't go in as a salesperson. You go in as a friendly person, a problem solver, offering to help them. It's almost impossible to get upset with someone offering to help you. You can use this to cold call residential areas or business areas. It's also easy on the people you call on. There's no pressure, so they can feel comfortable and open up to you.

Understand the laws of any kind of prospecting. Most people will not have any interest (need) for what you sell. That's to be expected; it's okay. You can't sell to people who don't have the problem your product or service solves, no matter how clever a sales talk. That's why I repeat the problem(s) three times, to make sure it registers. I never use any sales talk. When you walk in cold on people, they may not be totally focused on your first words. If they have that or a similar problem, you'll know immediately. Their eyes sort of light up and they start to ask questions. Bingo! A new suspect. Not a prospect just yet, but starting to look good.

The only problem I have in teaching this technique to new salespeople is that they keep sneaking in sales talk. *Don't*. It changes the entire nature of your call.

Success Method 11: People You Know

This is another area frequently overlooked by new salespeople. Not only do you know many more people than you may at first realize, but these people also have a huge circle of friends.

If you are married, sit down with your spouse when you prepare this list. Just write down as many answers to these questions as you can.

Who Do You Know?

- From your old job
- From school or college
- From religious worship
- Through your favorite sports or hobbies
- From civic activities
- Because you rent or own your home
- From other places you've lived
- Who sold you a car
- Who works at a gas station
- Who are your spouse's friends
- Through your children
- From lodge or club activities

- Who works where you buy groceries
- Who sells you clothes
- Who sells you shoes
- Who is a neighbor
- Who sold you office supplies
- Who is your dentist
- Who is your druggist
- Who is your doctor
- Who is your attorney
- Who was in your wedding party
- Who is your son's or daughter's scoutmaster
- Who gives music lessons
- Who took your family photograph
- Who is at your luncheon club
- Who does dry cleaning
- Who is in your local PTA
- Who sold you eyeglasses
- Who is a police officer
- Who is a firefighter
- Who sells you hardware
- Who does your printing
- Who heads your local Rotary, Lions, Kiwanis, etc.
- Who works in a bank or savings and loan
- Who handled your mortgage
- Who does your plumbing
- Who repairs your TV, etc.
- Who runs a beauty salon
- Who goes to the beauty salon
- Who runs a barbershop
- Who goes to the barbershop
- Who are your mom and/or dad's good friends
- Who does your tax returns
- From eating at a restaurant

With a little thought you can perhaps double this list. Some people resist preparing this kind of list, as if it's an embarrassment or improper thing to do, calling on friends and acquaintances. Here's a good way to ask people you know if they have an interest without appearing aggressive.

You say: "Hi, _____ , I just wanted to let you know I started a new career opportunity. I was wondering if you know anybody who (*state problem your product or service solves*)? If you know anyone who (*repeat problem your product or service solves*) I really believe I can help them. Who comes to mind?"

If they have an interest, they will start asking you questions. If not, you still have a shot at any friends they may have.

TWO PROSPECTING TACTICS I DON'T RECOMMEND

Advertising and direct mail are the first tactics newcomers to selling decide will make them rich. Rarely, and I do mean rarely, do they ever work. Even when they do, the returns are still often so minimal that you can't justify all the expense and time they required. Remember that time spent on these programs is time taken away from other, more fruitful prospecting. Time has a money value.

Let me tell you why newcomers get so excited about these tactics. They don't require going out and making in-person (or telephone) contact with strangers. People who have an aversion to making calls will immediately think that either direct mail or an advertisement is the way to go. For most business firms, especially small business firms, it's a good way to burn money.

Advertising

First, advertising. If you have a major consumer product, such as breakfast food, automobiles, and so on, certainly advertise. But, if you did have a major product, you wouldn't be reading this book.

There are numerous trade publications and business newspapers as well as consumer magazines and daily newspapers, all with large circulations, whose salespeople will say something like "We have over 450,000 readers per issue." That's so you think, "Gee, if I only get one-half of 1 percent to call me . . ." You suddenly get visions of huge amounts of business flowing to you, with no work on your part. Forget it, it won't happen.

To start off, publications always foster the myth that every issue is read by more than one reader, usually three. (To make it sound really accurate they say something like "2.7 readers per issue".) If you ask the same salesperson how many *issues* are printed, the answer will be 150,000. They won't tell you how many of those never leave the building where they were printed or how many are returned unsold from newsstands or how many are mailed to people who never wanted them in the first place.

Even if they did have the promised readership, most people in our society tune out most ads. They have to, there are just too many. As a small businessperson, your chances of a successful advertising campaign are very slim.

Radio and TV ads are just about the same. Small businesspeople don't have the financial means nor the employees trained in these areas of advertising to mount a successful campaign. There are some companies who specialize in selling this advertising to small business firms. It does not matter if it's print media, radio, or TV: As a small business stay away from these ads unless you actually see your competitors using them on a regular basis, over a long period of time.

What about people who sell ads in church directories, on billboards, and on plastic phone-book covers, to name a few of the novel deals running around? If you want to donate money to a local group sponsoring something like that, then do it. Consider it a donation, but don't expect a business return. Yellow-page phone directories not published by your local telephone company and so-called business directories are other examples of throwing money away for the small businessperson.

Real, authorized phone-company directories may be good for emergency businesses such as repair firms, medical and legal services, and so on. Pizza and home delivery ads do well. Other businesses frequently don't do very well. You may get calls, but often they are chiselers who are calling everybody in the book for the cheapest price. If you want real heartache, work that kind of crowd for a while.

Direct Mail

As with advertising, most people just tune out most direct mail. Advertising and direct mail is no place for amateurs. The art of advertising and the art of direct mail are the subjects of a great deal of study by very learned people. Entire college classes are taught on these topics and many well-educated people still go out and flop.

I hear people say that a good direct mail return is 4 percent or 5 percent. I've rarely seen any return close to that. One-half of 1 percent to 1 percent on a good mailing is a more realistic expectation. I can't even remember how many direct mailings I've seen go out and get *no return*—not just my own, but numerous companies that had so-called experts design the pieces and still drew nothing.

The only direct mail I've ever gotten any real mileage out of is when I have businesspeople send out small amounts every day, say 10 or 20, then follow up with a telemarketing call about five business days later. The mailing itself is almost valueless, but I do this when people have fears of making these calls and this acts as a sort of little crutch to help them get started. The real return comes from the telephone call.

5

Qualify and Succeed

Your success, your future in selling, depends on your ability to apply these principles of qualifying prospects. If you don't master this, and I mean *master* it, nothing else I can say or do will help.

THE 80–20 RULE

The 80–20 rule can be applied to many situations in life. Let me share it with you in terms of selling: 80 percent of all sales in any organization will be from 20 percent of its sales staff. That means that 80 percent of the salespeople are scrapping for only 20 percent of the available business. It really means that 80 percent of the salespeople are willing to settle for mediocrity. I don't want you to be in that 80 percent.

I've been a top 20-percent salesperson most of my life. However, when I started, I was an 80-percent person and stayed there for what seemed like a long time. (Time has a way of dragging when you work very long hours for little money.) It was only when I got really mad at not having enough money and at prospects who treated me with no respect that I applied the rules of selling I'm sharing with you in this book. Then and only then did the big bucks start coming in.

When I was a young salesperson, I subscribed to the theory that a good salesperson could sell anybody, anyplace, anytime. My first selling job was door-to-door sales at age 16 while on high-school vacation. To say that it was high-pressure selling would be an understatement. I later sold magazine subscriptions and cookware, all the same kind of high-pressure selling.

That was more years ago than I care to admit to. In the years following I've sold a lot of various products and services, most often in business ventures that I owned or was a partner in. Slowly but surely I began to see that being successful in sales relied less on high pressure and more on having in front of me a person who had a valid need for my product or service. I found that people who didn't respond to my sales pressure techniques had little or no real need for what I was selling. People who bought had strong reasons for doing so.

BEING AN 80-PERCENT SALESPERSON

For a few years I was one of those 80-percent salespeople. Sure I closed my share of sales, wrote many profitable sales contracts, but my income was always just a little above average, high enough to lull me into thinking I was doing okay. It was also low enough to leave me discontented.

It always bothered me that others were making more money doing the same exact job I did. For a while I retreated into the delusions of a salesperson who wasn't doing well.

Anyone in sales has heard this kind of twisted thinking among salespeople not selling successfully: "It's the economy," "Our prices are way too high," "We're not competitive," "The leads stink," "There's not enough leads." The excuse list is almost endless.

What it comes down to is people blaming outside situations for their inability to sell. Why? Because if they don't invent these excuses, they have to accept responsibility for their failure and many people can't. It's very hard to say "I don't have the courage to qualify a prospect's ability and willingness to buy," "I'm afraid to ask for an order," "I'm too lazy to spend a few hours every morning contacting new prospects," "I don't really understand fully what the benefits are of what I sell," "I don't have good selling skills," "I can't tell a good prospect from a bad one," or the big truth, "Selling overwhelms me."

It's a fact that people who are not doing well tend to become desperate. You see this in the actions of many salespeople. They are the 80-percent people.

Give them a lead and it's treated like gold. Whatever the prospect says or does is okay. Call him and he's busy? "Sure, so sorry to bother you, *sir*." He only talks to salespeople between 1:00 P.M. and 1:15 P.M. on the seventeenth day of every month? "Sure, no problem *sir*, I'll be sure to get back to you then." He wants to see your complete catalog, price lists, written testimonials, and a note from your doctor stating you carry no communicable diseases before he could even consider talking with you on the phone, let alone make an appointment with you? "Sure, no problem *sir*, I'll stay a few hours late at the office and copy everything you need. Then I'll drive 20 miles out of my way to ship it overnight." Make an appointment to see him and he's on vacation for two weeks when you arrive? "Sure, no problem *sir*, I'm sure a busy person like yourself . . ."

Sound exaggerated? You might be surprised (even shocked) at how close this is to real-life situations I've heard about when consulting and training salespeople. I'm always amazed at the amount of abuse some salespeople endure. It's almost a given that these are also the lowest-performing, least-successful salespeople in the organization.

FEAR OF PROSPECTING

Why would anybody put up with that mistreatment? The answer is fear. Fear that they may lose the prospect. Fear that they may not have anyone else to sell. And why might they not have anyone else to sell? Because they fear prospecting. Either they don't have the necessary skills to prospect and/or they have fears about asking people to buy something—a fear of rejection. It's this same fear that causes them to not qualify suspects. They don't want to ask someone if he or she is ready to buy, since that person might say no.

The good news is that, often, many such people have these feelings because no one has shown them the right way to sell. In most cases, solid sales training followed by real-life practice is the answer. When people first read these selling techniques they often have a problem seeing themselves actually doing them. But when they start doing, and not just reading, they see how really easy and productive the techniques are. Once they see the results these techniques produce, they can't believe they ever sold any other way. That's the purpose of this book, to show you the right way.

It's beyond the scope of this book to give an in-depth explanation of fear of rejection and low self-esteem, but if you or anyone you know has such concerns, have hope. Many other salespeople have also dealt successfully with this fear-of-rejection issue, whose root cause is low self-esteem. I have seen many promising sales careers go down the tubes because when the moment of truth came—calling on strangers—people simply could not do it on a sustained basis.

OTHER HELP

This self-esteem issue is directly tied to your success in selling. As a sales consultant and trainer I see this issue frequently. I want to share with you some ways you can get help should this book not cover the issue in enough depth.

Start with your library or bookstore. The keywords are assertiveness and self-esteem. There are many excellent tapes and books on these topics. Check in your community for any self-help study groups that meet to discuss these issues. If none of that does the trick, consider individual counseling from a professional therapist.

Please don't let self-esteem issues hurt your business. When you start on the road to improving your personal self-esteem, many other areas of your life will improve also—dramatically so. People sometimes don't say it, but everyone respects a person making a sincere effort to improve him- or herself. If this is an issue in your life, you are not alone. Have the courage to do something about it.

LET'S START TO QUALIFY OUR SUSPECTS

Rarely will you locate a suspect, qualify him or her to be a prospect, make a sales presentation, and then close the deal all at the same time. Usually when you find a suspect you qualify him or her to be a prospect and, if he or she is, you then set an appointment for the presentation.

It's important before you go on any sales call that you know there is a reasonable opportunity to make a sale. The failure of many people making sales calls is they get tired of prospecting so they make an appointment with the first available person. They hope they can convince this person to buy.

What happens is they spend a lot of time traveling, making a sales presentation, and then, because the prospect was really not interested enough to buy no matter what, fail to close. Salespeople spend all kinds of efforts on these kinds of prospects, using clever closing strategies, "guaranteed to work," that they read in books. They then leave beaten, tired, discouraged, and feeling as if they were a personal failure.

Many also feel that if they just had the right sales-closing technique, they might have had a sale. I see them time after time in my sales training classes. They are always seeking something new and different in sales strategies.

Here's That Old 80–20 Rule Again

What I tell them I will share with you in the next few paragraphs. As in my sales classes, some readers will believe me and some will not. The key to selling success is this: Successful salespeople spend nearly 80 percent of their time prospecting and qualifying, only 20 percent presenting.

The Five Magic Points of Qualification

I firmly believe that if you qualify a prospect on these five points and don't call on anyone who does not meet these criteria, you have completed 80 percent of the sale. When you focus your selling efforts on just these qualified prospects, your sales closing ratio will soar. The five points are:

1. *Problem.* Do they have a valid need (or strong desire) for what you sell? This means that the product or service you sell solves some sort of problem. Do they really have such a problem?

2. *Time Frame.* Need isn't enough. Assuming you can show them an acceptable solution, are they willing to buy now or within a reasonable period of time?

3. *Money.* Can they afford to pay your price?

4. *Decision Maker(s)*. If you set an appointment, will all decision makers be present?

5. *Judgment*. By what standards will they judge the purchase of your product or service? Does it need to meet some criteria? What?

Here are a few sample questions to qualify a suspect.

Time Frame

"Mr. _____ , assuming I could show you an acceptable solution to your problem, would you be willing to go ahead immediately?"

Can They Afford You?

"Ms. _____ , our _____ run anywhere between $ _____ and $ _____ . Which of these prices would be closest to your budget?"

Decision Makers

"Mr. _____ , other than yourself, who else would be required to make a buying decision?"

Now before anyone gets all excited, let me acknowledge that many sales are made each and every day by people who don't follow this or any other pattern of qualification. I certainly know that. But you purchased this book for a reason. One of them had to be how to sell effectively. What I am showing you here is how to sell both effectively and consistently, not by blind luck. This simply means that prospecting, which is the hardest part of selling, is where you need to spend the most time. There are no shortcuts to this rule. That's why many people have a big problem accepting what I say. They are not happy prospecting and wish someone would just mail them enough leads to exist. Since they don't like to prospect they have a problem accepting my analysis.

When I was in the security-alarm industry we made calls on new prospects with a list of what we needed to know before we would ever agree to come back.

Who, besides this person, made a final buying decision?

If this was not the only decision maker, when can I interview the decision maker(s)?

Did they have a realistic budget set aside for this purchase, now?

Assuming I could provide them with a system that would meet their requirements and budget, would they purchase immediately? If not, why not?

These were hard questions but I always asked, and kept asking, until I got hard answers. I was frequently amazed at the number of prospects who looked perfectly good on paper who were really nonbuyers or long shots at the very best.

The day I went from being an 80-percent salesperson, barely make a living, to a 20-percent salesperson, making big bucks, was the day I decided not to spend a large amount of time on any prospect who didn't qualify as someone I had a reasonable chance of selling in the reasonable future.

The Qualification Questionnaire

When I first learned sales, I was taught to ask questions of the prospect to determine if he or she qualified as to ability to pay, need for our product, interest level, and so on. My company had developed a whole series of excellent questions to slip into the initial conversation so that I did not spend a lot of time with people who, for whatever reason, were not prone to buy.

Unfortunately, I'd get nervous and forget part of the questions. Then I'd just go ahead with a sales presentation, which was very time consuming. Nearly every time I'd get all involved trying to sell people who were really unqualified and were never going to buy anything. Of course they'd never tell me that. To allow themselves to feel good after wasting my time, they gave me reasons for not buying that would make me look bad. Our quality was bad, prices were too high, service was lousy, company wasn't qualified, and so on. I can still remember a few who were downright nasty. My self-esteem hit rock bottom.

Each time I'd promise myself I'd better qualify prospects, but soon after I would start backsliding and repeating the same bad experiences.

I finally decided that my memory, when I was under the pressure of selling, just did not always come through. I sat down and typed out the questions I needed to ask. At the end of each question I typed a long blank line in which to write the answers. In addition, I made space to fill in the full name, job title, and company information about the prospect I was calling on. Some people in companies I would call on would be vague about their name or job title, or if anyone else besides them were required for a buying decision. They'd act a little abrupt so I was afraid to ask twice.

At this point I decided to heck with them. I felt I had every right to ask until I got the answer. I realized that the only people who acted like this were the ones who never purchased. I decided to make it a rule never to make a sales presentation until all questions were answered. Common sense and previous experience with my good customers told me that by asking questions, I was showing a serious interest in helping a prospect solve a problem.

People with problems never seemed to mind answering questions; only the ones who had little or no interest acted cagey. I realized at that point that the questionnaire itself was a fantastic qualifier. It eliminated people who had little interest but might have been curious or had nothing else going, were bored and wanted entertainment, and so on. I made copies of the questionnaire and filled one out with prospects before I made any sales presentation or price quotes. It worked wonders. Here's how I'd introduce it:

"Mr. _____, I'm sure you value your time as much as I value mine. Before I explain how we can (*benefit*), I'd like to ask you a few questions. The answers will help me focus on helping you achieve (*benefit*) in the most efficient manner possible. Okay?"

"How Much Is It?"

I saved this item until last in this chapter on purpose. If you learn this little gem and nothing else by reading my book, you'll have come out ahead.

Prospects frequently ask, "How much is it?" The rule, carved in stone, is you refuse to quote any price until you have made an appointment for a sales presentation. You then deal with the question at the appointment, after the sales presentation.

There's an old saying many experienced salespeople know very well, "When the price is too high, the interest is too low." If you don't spend some time in a sales presentation with prospects, they can't possibly know all the benefits of doing business with you. They know all salespeople make big claims. You have to convince them that your claimed benefits are real. That takes a sales presentation.

When people first meet you (or speak to you by telephone), they may have an interest in your product or service, but it's usually fairly casual. At this point, they know so little about you they don't know what to ask in order to decide if they will see you, so they ask price questions. Since they really don't understand how you can help them at this stage, any price you quote will be too high.

You can be offering $100 bills for $50 and someone will say, "Sorry, can't afford it" or "We don't have any more budget left this year" or "Your competitor down the street sells them cheaper." The minute you start out with any price before a presentation, you invite rejection.

There's only one way to answer: "The price varies, I wouldn't know until we sit down. I will promise this, if it doesn't (*insert your main benefit here*), it costs you nothing. I can see you at ____ or at ____ . Which would be better?"

Most people will respond positively if they have an interest. Occasionally someone will try to bait you into quoting a price, "Just give me a ballpark figure" or "How about a guesstimate?" Politely refuse. Keep going back to the benefits and ask again for an appointment . They are trying to judge you using price alone. Don't fall into the trap. I promise you, you can't win.

6

Sales Presentations That Make People Eager to Buy

Of all the failures most people make in sales calls, the failure to have a predetermined sales presentation tops the list. Many people, especially newcomers to selling, will go out on a perfectly good sales lead and say whatever they feel appropriate at the time. They have no plan, no thought as to what they want or expect out of the interview. They just wing it and then complain when things go bad. You must know, in advance, what you plan to say to the person(s) and what you expect to accomplish.

Forget the "I want a sale from the interview." That's too broad. Many sales take multiple calls to close, many sales require taking additional steps to complete, perhaps additional appointments with other buying influences. Sometimes sales calls are simply to gather information for a proposal, give a quote, or just see if the prospect is serious. It's not realistic to expect to sell everyone you call on. It is very realistic to know what you want in specific terms before you ever see the prospect.

STEP 1: SALES RULES OF THE ROAD

The laws of common sense apply to sales appointments. The way you dress, speak, and carry yourself all have bearing on how well or poorly you'll do in your sales interview. Prospects will judge you even if they are trying not to. There is a great deal of truth to the saying, "Make a good first impression."

The way you dress should be very business-like. You want prospects to think of you as successful and very professional. Sometimes you'll call on a business account where the company bosses run around in casual clothes, or in people's homes where they dress casual, but that's no reason for you to. Keep in mind that people like to buy from solid, dependable sources. You must look the part to instill confidence.

For men, usually a dark-colored business suit or sport coat with coordinated trousers, white shirt, necktie, dress shoes, a recent haircut, nails either manicured or at least clean, and shoes polished. For women, a dark-colored suit or dress, well-groomed hair, no garish nail polish or jewelry, no sexy clothes. The key here is to dress conservatively.

Author John T. Malloy wrote a book several years ago that is a real classic on how to (and why to) dress in business to make an excellent impression. It's called *Dress for Success*. He wrote a second version for women, *Women's Dress for Success*. I'm sure your local library has a copy you can read. It's critical to look the part. Especially if you are new to much of this.

Never accept an alcoholic beverage, smoke, or chew gum on sales calls. Never mind what the prospect is doing. You're there to sell. Generally it's okay to accept a nonalcoholic beverage if you are offered one.

STEP 2: A LITTLE SCHMOOZING

When you arrive at a prospect's home or office on a sales appointment, you must take charge, that is, be assertive enough to control the conversation and the interview.

I've found that a little small talk (a few minutes at most) relaxes people. A comment about traffic, weather, local sports team, or anything else where you may share a common area of agreement helps. People like to do business with people they like and if you have a small common bond, it makes them feel a little more comfortable about you.

A word of warning: A little small talk goes a long way. Your prospect may have interrupted something else important to see you. Don't waste valuable interview time; prospects will also respect you for that. If the prospect gets long winded, then you need to be assertive enough to get the sales interview politely back on track. Finally, no politics, ethnic remarks, dirty jokes, or sexist comments belong in your interviews, ever.

STEP 3: REQUALIFY YOUR PROSPECT BEFORE YOUR PRESENTATION (WHY AM I HERE?)

I carry a sales qualification questionnaire with me on all sales calls. I described to you in the last chapter how it came about. I've typed out a list of things I need to know in order to sell them. After a little small talk, I say something like, "Mr. Prospect, I'm sure you value your time as much as I do mine. In order for me to (*benefit of what you sell*) in the most efficient manner, I'll need to ask you a few questions, okay?"

The first step in qualifying a prospect is to know what a buyer of your product or service looks like. For instance, here's a personal example I use right now. I sell sales training and seminar programs (yes, I still sell; it's the part of this business I enjoy the most). I know from reviewing past customers that these are four characteristics (of several) of a buyer of sales training. They must be present in each and every interview:

1. They have multiple salespeople.
2. They are not happy with present results.
3. They can afford to spend money on a solution.
4. They have the authority to authorize purchase of my services.

Some prospects will allow you to make a sales call on them not really understanding what you sell and what it costs. Other prospects will see you because they have nothing better to do. Some will see you because they want to get all the details and present it to their boss, hoping to earn brownie points in the process. Still others will interview you because they either are now or plan to be selling what you do and they want to see what you sell so they can go out and do it themselves. None of them really mean you any harm, but you can't earn a living spending valuable selling time with people who will never buy.

By knowing what I want, I can effectively ask questions of prospects to determine if they have a valid need for my services. For instance, I might ask, "How many salespeople do you employ?" If they give me a specific answer, then I know what the sales potential is. If, however, the answer is evasive, or they become defensive or they have no salespeople, a red flag goes up.

I might ask, "What problems are you having with your sales staff that you might consider training to correct?" A straight answer would be something specific such as poor closing skills, salespeople not developing their own leads, poor motivation, and so on. Should I hear, "We really don't have any problems," that concerns me. While some people are cautious about revealing their problems immediately, especially to someone they don't know well, they must somehow acknowledge how you can help. Otherwise, there's no point in going on. I would do some additional gentle probing. Here are a few examples:

"Are you saying then that no one in your organization could benefit from hearing me? How then might someone like myself be of help to you?" or "If I had a magic wand and could make any changes in your sales staff performance you wanted, what would that be?"

Let's say the prospect looks okay to this point. Now I need to know what kind of money he or she has to solve the problem. I know I can't do business where the total sale is under $2,500. It is just not cost effective. Here are questions I might ask a prospect:

"Mary, what sort of budget do you have set aside to address this problem?" or "Jack, our training packages start out between $2,500 to $4,500 for basic, $5,000 to $10,000 for custom design, and our most-detailed would be in the $15,000 range. Where do you see yourself, dollarwise?"

If he responds to the basic, I'll say: "On the basic package do you see yourself closer to the $2,500 range or the $4,500 range?"

If he is at the low end, $2,500, I'll try to make sure he has that much: "Jack, do I hear you saying that you have $2,500 set aside right now to deal with this issue?" I put the words "right now" in on purpose. If the prospect doesn't have it, he or she will start to hedge answers.

Unacceptable Answers

The prospect must say yes to me in a way I can believe. Here are some answers you should never accept:

"Money's not a problem." "If I see what I like, I can get the money." "Let's worry about what you sell first before we talk money." "That's none of your business."

Don't fear offending people by asking them if they can afford what you sell. Your selling time is valuable to you and you have every right to know if you take your time to make a complete sales presentation, they have the ability to buy. In my years of selling I've found that people who are sincerely interested never get offended if you ask a legitimate question about money, even if it turns out they can't afford you.

It's only the people who know in advance they are not going to buy anything who become defensive or evasive. They are the ones who get upset and are trying, with aggressiveness, to cover up their inability or unwillingness to buy. They are either insincere time wasters, have no money, or don't have the authority to buy. Consider yourself lucky to find that out early in the interview.

I remember coming back to my office one day several years ago, depressed because some guy had gotten bent out of shape when I inquired at a first interview about his ability to purchase. My brother Bob, who was my business partner at the time, had a different viewpoint. "Look at it this way, you could have spent hours doing a proposal, then had the guy pull this stunt. At least you're free to concentrate on productive business." On his way out the door of my office he turned and said, "Actually, he did you a favor by showing you what he was really like, up front." Bob was right.

Think about it. If you go into a place of business and you are really interested in something, would you actually get mad if asked what price range you were looking for?

TED'S SALES RULE

I don't give sales
presentations unless
all decision makers
are present.

Who's the Real Buyer?

Back to my example. The question I'd ask next (assuming I had acceptable answers to the first two) would be:

"Assuming, after our presentation, you feel we're right for you, who, besides yourself, would be required to make a decision to buy today?" I stick in the word "today" on purpose. This is a sales call, not a social visit. I want them to know that.

If I find another party is involved, I want this person present at the interview. Sometimes in companies a person without the authority to buy will take up a lot of your time, hoping to present your program to a higher authority. I learned from hard and bitter experience that most times the higher authority has little or no interest and you may have spent hours working on a nearly hopeless situation.

Just as in the money step, listen carefully for evasive answers. If you find out the person you are speaking with is not the decision maker, be careful to include them in your statements. That way they don't feel you are cutting them out. I always suggest a "meeting with the three of us."

If, however, they try to get information from me or a sales presentation so they can present it to the decision maker, I always decline. If necessary, I'll leave. I never waste time on nonbuyers. The only story they will take to the real buyer is your price. Without a sales presentation, your price will always be too high. Never waste time with people who don't have the authority to sign your contract and write you a check.

What if you sell individuals, not companies? It's all the same, just reword the questions. One important issue: When selling to married couples or people living together, always have both present. Most couples feel that spending money is a joint decision. The minute one makes a decision without the other present, the one who was left out gets hurt and angry. Often a family fight ensues, then they make up, blame you for the whole thing, and, of course, cancel.

Stop

Any time you have an appointment at someone's home or business where two decision makers are supposed to be there and only one is available, stop. Reschedule if the reason this person give sounds sincere, but no matter what he or she says or does, don't make a sales presentation. Spend your selling time with someone who can make a decision.

Words to Qualify... Immediately!

During any sales interview, be wary of what I call meaningless words. People use them to lull you into a sense of false security. That way you won't ask the hard questions and maybe discover this person isn't the hot prospect you thought. Here are a few examples of meaningless words, along with my responses in parentheses:

"I'm just looking." (For what?) "I might be interested." (Under what circumstances?) "Sounds okay." (Does that mean you'll buy?) "We'll give you every consideration." (What exactly does that mean?) "We'll think it over." (Think what over?) "It looks good." (Does that mean you'd like to order now or you just like the color?)

These are frequently insincere statements made to mislead you into thinking whatever it is you want to think. The prospect has made no promises, just stroked you along a little. When I hear people say these things I ask the questions you see in parentheses. Always qualify any statement that really isn't clear.

It's surprising how quickly prospects clarify their statements. Of course, some people are ready to buy when they make those statements. By asking these qualifying questions, I then know if I should proceed to a close. As you will learn later, when people have made a subconscious buying decision, you must stop selling and close the order. Otherwise, as you babble on, they can change their minds again.

TED'S SALES RULE

Most people don't need
or even want to know
everything you know
about what you sell.

STEP 4: TALK BENEFITS

Features Alone Mean Little if Anything

There is a secret to successful selling. People who make a big income learn it; those who don't, don't. The secret is always speaking to prospects in terms of what's in it for them. Amateur salespeople stress product features. The moneymaking pros rarely do. They always talk about how the prospect will benefit, the end result of the product's features.

When you purchased your car, did you require a detailed explanation of how the thing works before you'd buy it? How about your TV set? Refrigerator? Do you have the foggiest idea, right now, of how these items really work? Do you care?

Then why did you make these or similar purchases? Because of what these items could do for you: the benefits. A lot of product knowledge can wreck your sales. Nobody buys anything based on product knowledge, despite the lies they will tell you.

The Buying Motive

People buy because of what they will get out of it. A car purchase means safety to some, looking like an important person to others. To some, a new TV means saving money by being entertained at home instead of going out a lot; to another, it may be a way for a mom to keep the kids quiet while she gets housework done.

That's why it's important to ask lots of questions about how someone will use whatever you sell. To find the buying motive, ask questions, lots of them. Many people will be cagey about the true buying motive. "Just looking around" or "Thought I'd see what's out there" are vague answers that need to be probed.

Buying is an emotional decision. Facts and reason have little to do with buying.

The Bridge

Whenever you give someone a fact on your product or service, it only has meaning if you attach it to some benefit that the prospect can relate to. A bridge is simply the few words you use to connect the fact you've just mentioned to the benefit it represents.

A common bridge is "which means." In a sales sentence it would sound like this, "This model car has a 26-gallon gas tank, which means a lot fewer stops at gas stations." You need lots of different bridges so you don't keep repeating yourself. When selling, you need to reword your bridges differently so it doesn't sound boring. Some alternate bridges: "this allows you to ... " or "because of that ... " or "with that feature you can ... " As a practice exercise, write out eight or 10 bridges you can use. How many more can you think of?

The Rule

Never mention any feature of your product or service without telling the prospects the benefit it represents *to them*.

The Benefit

A benefit is simply what your product or service will do to benefit the prospects when they purchase. I know some very successful people who never even mention anything technical about what they sell. All they do is ask tons of questions about the prospects' needs and discuss how they can benefit them with their product or service.

There's only one reason someone buys: for what they can get out of it (the benefit). For some, a car means dependable transportation; to others, a flashy model means getting noticed. A new TV means saving money by being entertained at home instead of going out to some. To a mom it may be a way to keep the kids quiet while she gets housework done. This is why it's so important to ask lots of questions in Step 2. You not only want to qualify people, you need to know why they are interested in the first place, what potential problems you'll be solving. If people don't really have a problem, they have no need. No need means no buy.

It's Really Simple to Talk Benefits. Here's How!

Mention a feature of whatever it is you sell, then add on the words, "which means," then simply tell them how it benefits them.

"The car has a 26-gallon gas tank, *which means* you'll need to stop less frequently at gas stations."

"The computer has a 500-megabyte hard drive, *which means* you'll have plenty of room for all the newest software and your records."

"The cellular telephone folds up to fit into a shirt pocket, *which means* you can take a telephone with you, conveniently, wherever you go."

Now you try it. I want you to write down four features about your own product or service. Add the words "which means" to each, then write down the benefits they provide for your prospects. Stop reading and try it.

If I were a salesperson selling the cellular phone, I'd start talking to prospects about how they could go places and still keep their telephone communication with them. I'd ask them how they might use it. The idea is to get them to see themselves taking advantage of the benefits. Nobody really cares how something folds up. But they sure might care about being able to keep in communication.

STEP 5: THE QUALIFIER

How Can You Tell What Benefits
Prospects Really Care About? Ask!

In my experience, most salespeople usually have enough product knowledge to talk themselves out of a sale. If you are a business owner acting as your own salesperson, you really have the ability to talk your way to nowheresville. A qualifier is simply asking a prospect if the benefit you just stated would be of importance to him or her. Without a qualifier you have no way to know when to stop selling and start closing the sale.

Selling is like a pendulum swinging on a clock. During your sales presentation, people will start to decide they want to buy. If you don't stop talking and go into a close, they will start to reconsider the initial buying decision and then you can't close them.

Remember, people will be buying for some need. You may know 10 or 15 features and benefits about what you sell, but to your prospects, only one or two of those matter. The rest are actually boring to them. The big problem is, of the 10 or 15 benefits you may know, you'll never have a real idea of what their buying motive is unless you ask questions.

After each benefit, just ask if that is important to them. If they say no, then don't bring it up again. If they say yes, then you have hit a hot button and need to use a trial close.

Here are a few qualifiers. "How does that sound?" or "Can you see yourself using that feature?" or "Would that be important to you?" or "Do you think your family (boss) would like that?" As an exercise, see how many more you can write down.

Another method is to restate the benefit and end with questions such as: "Isn't it?" "Wouldn't you?" "Doesn't it?" "Does that make sense?" "Sound like something you would benefit from?" "Is that what you have in mind?" "Would you find that important?"

Power Sales Units—Putting It All Together

A power sales unit is simply a sentence containing a feature, bridge, benefit, and qualifier. Because all of this can sometimes get long, two or even three sentences are used.

Here's an example:

"This copy machine has a double-sized capacity toner drum, which means your employees don't have to stop their regular work to fill the machine very frequently. Here's the specification sheet showing how long you can go between fill-ups. Would this feature be of any importance to you?"

STEP 6: WHAT'S THE BUYING MOTIVE?

Let's say you sell a product or service that has 10 really decent features about it. Most people buy for one or maybe two reasons at most. You may (I hope you do) know 10, 15, even 20 features and benefits about your product or service.

If you tell people about all of them, you'll bore them and lose them. You should now have a clue from the initial questionnaire in Step 3. You can confirm what's important by giving them a feature and benefit, then ask, "Wouldn't that be important to you?" If they say yes, continue in that area. On the other hand, if they say it isn't a really very important issue, drop it.

TED'S SALES RULE

People don't buy
for your reasons.

They buy for theirs.

If you keep trying to sell features and benefits that have no valid meaning to your prospects, they tune you out. Never just start talking at random about what you sell. Find out why you are there. Why are they spending their valuable time to see you? What are they hoping you can do for them? If you can't get the answer to that question, stop everything until you do.

Remember, you may think your clever words and sales skills got you this appointment. In truth you have found people with a problem who are hoping you have a solution. That's why they are taking time to see you. They hope as much as you do what you sell can solve some problem or issue for them. Unfortunately many people get a little cagey about admitting any problem. It takes skill and practice asking questions to uncover many people's real needs. The best salespeople in the world are also the best questioners.

STEP 7: PROVE IT

Making a lot of unsubstantiated claims for your product or service will leave most people cold. Television today is filled with all kinds of commercials promising all kinds of benefits, many of them greatly exaggerated. Most people you try to sell are not really going to be impressed by fantastic claims unless you can prove them. You have to prove in some way to prospects you are able to do what you promise.

As a consultant, when I visit sales organizations in trouble I often find they rarely if ever have a formal sales presentation, or if they do, they don't insist the salesperson use it. The methods shown in this step are incredibly powerful selling tools.

Here are eight methods that are successfully used. Use as many as reasonably applies to what you sell.

Demonstrate

Some products and services can be demonstrated. A retired auto-industry salesman told me how a major plate glass company sold manufacturers on shatterproof glass years ago. It consisted of two layers of glass with a clear, plastic-like substance sandwiched in the middle, to hold the glass together. Up to that point, flying glass in car accidents was a big danger.

The salesperson would walk into a buyer's office and set a piece of shatterproof glass on the buyer's desk. The buyer of course would assume it was regular sheet glass. "You know how big a danger flying glass is in car accidents, right?" the salesperson would ask.

"Sure," the buyer would say.

The salesperson would say, "I want you to see something. Watch this!" As he spoke he'd pull a hammer out of his coat, raise it overhead and smash the glass. Most buyers, expecting flying glass, would scream and dive for the floor. They tell me the plate glass company had one heck of a year, with record sales, all from that little demonstration.

When I was in the security-alarm industry, we were selling in essence a service. Sure, there were products used to install a security system, but most people were not buying because of the product.

They were concerned with protecting themselves from burglary and fire with our systems.

Our most effective demonstration was of the service. We'd take clients into the central alarm station where the emergency calls were handled. It was impressive, heavily guarded, and computerized. It was proof we could handle their security reliably.

When you sell a service, demonstrating a benefit becomes a bit of a challenge. I know a salesperson who sells insurance. She wants her prospects to realize that the cost is low. She will put two packs of chewing gum on the table and say, "For just the price of two packs a day, you can provide this valuable protection for your family, Mr. Jones. Certainly they are worth that small an investment, aren't they?"

Photographs are another way to demonstrate some services. A landscape service has before and after pictures of the work they have done. It's a much more powerful way than just talking about recent jobs. With pictures, people can see with their own eyes the results your service can provide.

One caution about pictures: Unless you are really good with a camera, invest in a professional photographer. You need good-sized prints, properly exposed, and in sharp focus to make a good impression.

If you sell anything that can be demonstrated, do so.

Have Prospects Do Something with Their Hands

We had a complete security-alarm system wired up in an attaché case for demonstration purposes. It was an alarm-control panel, a siren unit, a touch keypad to activate and deactivate the unit (it looked like the Touch-Tone buttons on your telephone), and a small door frame with a miniature door that opened and closed.

When I'd bring it in, I'd make a big deal out of looking for an electrical outlet to plug it in. I'd hand the cord to the prospect to do it. I'd describe how the keypad worked and then ask the prospect to set it. I'd then ask the prospect to open the little door. The siren was loud and they'd usually flinch a little as it activated. I'd shut the siren off and ask the prospect to pull the electrical plug from the wall. I'd then have them repeat arming and activating the system and seeing that, even without electrical power, the alarm would work. There was a lot more to it, but you get the idea. The prospect was actively involved in the entire demonstration, a part of it, not a bystander.

It's very effective if anything you sell can be handed to a prospect at some point, or if he or she can be a part of any demonstration. I know people who will hand a legal pad and calculator to the prospect and ask him or her to write down key numbers and do calculations that show how the prospect benefits.

Testimonials: Getting Good Ones

There are two secrets to getting good testimonials. First, write them for the prospect. Most people who don't mind writing one don't really know what to say, so they promise you one and then never send it. Here's exactly what I'd say to get my testimonials.

Me: "Mr. Prospect, are you pleased with our security system? Did we do everything I promised we'd do?"

Prospect: "Yes, we really like it. You kept your word."

Me: "Great, I'm glad you're satisfied. I was wondering if you could do me a small favor?"

Prospect: "What?"

Me: "We like to keep a file of letters from a select few of our better customers to show others we do good work. I'd like to invite you to be a part of that file. All I'll need is a few words from you on your letterhead telling us what you think about our system and our service."

Prospect: "Well, I guess it won't hurt."

At this stage I'd suggest to him to take out a few sheets of his stationery, tell me what to say, and I'd have our company secretary type it up and bring it back for his signature. I'd offer to word it for him also if he wished. Notice how I stated my request. I identified him as one of a select few of our better customers. I made him feel honored to be asked for a testimonial.

The second secret to getting a testimonial is timing. If you ask before your product is delivered or service started, people don't know you well enough. If you wait a long time after, they cool down and it's much harder to obtain one. The best time is after they have enjoyed whatever you sell for a week or so. I used to make a specific sales call just for that purpose.

Samples/Free Trials

Some companies sell products or services that lend themselves to sampling and/or a free trial offer. It's not a good idea to do this with everyone. However, if you identify a prime prospect, make a sales call, and find he or she is sincerely interested, then for certain products or services it may be an effective option. I've heard of services such as pagers, telephone answering, and so on, allowing people a one- or two-week trial.

For instance, some office-machine companies will install a copier for one or two weeks on a trial basis to qualified prospects. If they like the machine, they keep it. If not, it goes back. In such a case I'd certainly have a written agreement stating who pays for usable materials if any, who would be financially responsible for any damages, and that they acknowledge the unit was my property on loan only and I had the right to pick it up. I've heard of a few cases where equipment came back badly misused and other cases where they couldn't get back in to pick up the equipment. There are, unfortunately, some unscrupulous people. Be selective with on-site demonstrations.

I know one company who got past all that. They offered in ads a 30-day in-office demonstration without obligation to buy, with the specific understanding that after 30 days, the demonstration unit was sold to the prospect and stayed there. What the company did was actually sell the machine, getting financing approved and purchase contracts signed. The purchase contract had a special clause that said the buyer could return the machine without any payments at the 30-day point. After that, it became a regular sale.

Another kind of sampling is simply to give people sample products. Usually this applies to edibles. For instance, one caterer I know brings slices of her famous chocolate torte cake to the sales call in a sealed plastic food container. (She checks first to make sure the prospect likes chocolate.) When she walks into a client's home or office she asks the client to please be seated. She then makes a big production out of placing a place mat, napkin, and real plate and fork in front of the client, who doesn't have a clue as to what she is doing. She then makes another production out of opening the container and, with a beautiful silver cake server, serves a small sliver to the prospect.

"One taste is all I ask," she'll say sweetly. Of course, she has every confidence in the great taste of her product. She also knows to serve a small slice so everyone wishes for a little more. The smallness of the slice and the way she handles the serving as a big production makes the cake seem even more valuable.

These prospects may talk to other caterers and see other cakes, but they never will forget this production.

Deferred Billing

Deferred billing is similar to the idea of giving samples. Here you might sell prospects and not bill them for, say, 30 days. It's usually with the understanding that if they are not satisfied they can cancel without paying anything or pay some minimal amount. It's a way to tell people you have so much confidence in your offering you are not afraid to let them try it.

A word of warning: If you have a small business, remember that deferred billing and sampling promotions as I've described are not without risk. They usually mean you won't be seeing very much money coming in the door right away, while the cost of sales and overhead continue. Unless you have a substantial cash reserve to carry you over this period of time, I wouldn't do it.

Further, there are some people who will take advantage of such offers, knowing they plan to cancel no matter how good the product or service is. You have to expect that. Always have such programs in writing and reviewed by your attorney. Your customers need a clear, written understanding, up front.

Facts and Statistics

If you have a product or service you are making claims for, think about how you might be able to locate statistics or facts to prove these claims. Some of the most common sources for accurate facts and statistics, all at very low or no cost, are:

1. *Libraries.* Your local public library for starters. I've found that the larger library systems have extensive collections of valuable business data on numerous subjects.

2. *Colleges.* Many colleges have their own library. They also can be a great resource.

3. *Manufacturers—Service Suppliers.* If you sell products from a manufacturer or service from a larger service provider, check with their marketing departments. They may have done the exact research you are doing and be able to make it available to you.

Even if these resources don't have exactly what you need, chances are they'll be able to direct you to places that do.

Once you locate the data, you need to reproduce them in some form to carry with you on sales calls. Here are some ways I've handled this in the past with success. I copied newspaper articles to fit an 8½" x 11" sheet. At the top I write "Reprint from (name of publication)." I show the date of the reprint. If it's an article that only has a small mention of what I want to emphasize, I circle the appropriate remarks with a black felt-tip marker or a brightly colored highlighter. That way the readers' eyes travel immediately to the copy I want them to see.

For charts and graphs I try to reproduce them the same way. If that's not practical, I have them redone. None of this is as difficult as it sounds. With modern computer desktop publishing methods it's relatively simple. If you own such equipment, you can do it yourself. In some locations you can rent time on computers and do your own work. If you don't go that route, some of the quick-printing and copy shops will do desktop publishing as an additional service. Also, check at colleges for part-timers or ads in the paper for people working out of their homes. A word of caution: Always ask to see samples of their work before you assign.

Warranties and Limited Warranties

We live in an age of warranties. To most people a warranty means if you don't like the product, you get your money back. Perhaps in your business, that's the best policy.

However, if you read the fine print in most warranties, they do not promise that at all. Warranties are limited in what they guarantee and in what happens if the guarantee is exercised by the buyer. Not all guarantees offer complete satisfaction.

Select something you are strong at in your business and guarantee it. For instance, "We guarantee you'll be completely satisfied with the installation or we'll do it over again, free." or "We'll have our service person at your site within 24 hours or you don't pay for the service call." Consider offering a replacement or repair-only guarantee, or with a service, additional no-charge service, not money back. It's less costly and gives you a second chance to satisfy the customer. Give money back and customers go elsewhere.

Offering a warranty will further convince some prospects to do business with you. If you're not sure what to warranty, do a survey of your present customers and find out what their biggest concern is when buying what you sell. Consider how you can in some way warranty whatever is mentioned most frequently.

Be careful to warranty something that you honestly don't feel is a problem. All warranties should be reviewed and approved by your attorney before you offer them.

Products or Services in Use

On occasion we would take prospects to visit customers (after getting permission from our customers) who had previously purchased our service and let the prospects see the system in action. Save this for the really important prospects you want to impress. (Don't visit the same firm more than once or twice—you don't want to annoy your customer.)

STEP 8: CREATE A SENSE OF URGENCY

Potential Buyers Become Eager to Own; Tire Kickers Will Either Become Potential Buyers or Back Off!

You may be wondering when you actually quote a price. Remember, earlier we qualified prospects as to ability to pay, but no price was quoted. At this point they would have only a vague idea as to price.

TED'S SALES RULE

People always want
what they believe is
in short supply or
hard to get.

The best situation is to have them ask you. If they ask before you have gone into at least a third of your sales presentation I'd say something such as, "That's a good question, I'll address that in just a moment."

On the other hand, if they are past the one-third point and ask price, I'd qualify with a question such as, "I think you can already see yourself owning this, is that a fair statement?" What you must do is make sure they have seen enough to be convinced your product or service is of value to them. You don't want the decision to be based on price alone.

A good salesperson, a 20-percent salesperson, will condition his or her prospect on price and also will instill some sense of urgency. If people feel they can get it anytime, what's the rush? You need to understand and apply this strategy. Following are examples of three strategies designed to make people feel a need to buy. Consider how you can apply one of them to what you sell.

Strategy 1—It May Not Be Available

Have you ever gone in a store for a closer look at something you saw in a store window and the salesperson says, "Gee, I think we're sold out, that's the last one. I can check the stockroom for your size if you want." Suddenly you feel a sense of loss. You hear yourself asking the salesperson to check the stockroom. A good salesperson would add, "If I have one left, do you want to buy it?"

A banker may say, "If you're planning to do something today I'd better check the rates to see if they are still that low. Do you want me to go ahead if I can get that rate?"

A car salesperson may say, "I don't know if I can sell this one, it's our only one left to show. Do you want me to ask the sales manager?" If the potential buyer says to check, the car salesperson then says, "Should I put a temporary hold on it?"

A real-estate salesperson might say, "I'd love to show you that property, providing somebody hasn't put in an offer on it. It's really a nice property and others have been looking at it also. Would you like me to check?"

Strategy 2—The Right Way to Use Price Increase

A lot of salespeople try this and it fails because when they do it, it is done so halfheartedly the prospects see through it. They usually say it *after* they have presented a price quote and *after* the prospect turns them down. It's one of those desperate, last-thought stabs at bringing back a dead sale. At that point, it makes the salesperson look pathetic. Here's a more positive, believable way.

Before you quote a price, early on in the interview, say "I've got a small problem. These prices I quote you may go up a little bit by the time you get around to making a buying decision. Not a lot, maybe 10 percent." Don't say anymore about it. When you get to the price, just say, "At today's rates, your total investment would be _____ ." Don't try to close on the "Buy now before the price goes up" theme. It makes what you said sound more valid, like you have no control over it.

If someone is serious, he or she will start some conversation about "How long can you guarantee that price." *Don't* answer. Instead, qualify how serious the prospect may be. Ask, "I don't really know. How soon were you planning to buy?" Don't ever check (or pretend) to check on holding a guaranteed price without a commitment from the prospect. Simply say, "I can't call my boss unless you're serious." The prospect has now walked into a trial close.

Strategy 3—Time Availability

Frequently, consultants, trainers, time-share programs, and so on use this tactic. Again, this works only at a certain point in a sales process. When you get to the stage of discussing price and delivery of the service you get the prospect to decide (not you) when he or she wants the service. Again you say, "Let me check my calendar." You come back with, "Sorry, I have a partial commitment on that time." If you've waited until the prospect has decided he or she really wants that time because it's convenient, you hold some power. Do this too early and it isn't very good. Again, if the prospect shows a desire for that time, require a firm commitment before you will "see if I can shift things around."

While all these are really trial sales-closing techniques, they must be started early on in the sales process, then brought up again at the end. I've done this at the start of a sales process with really interested prospects and never got to the presentation stage. The minute they thought they couldn't get what they wanted, they purchased to make sure they could!

STEP 9: HOW TO QUOTE A PRICE

The way you present the price is critical to the sales process. Many times, people have very little idea of what anything costs. Unless the salesperson presents a little psychological conditioning, the "price is too high" objection starts up immediately. The wise salesperson will prepare the prospect for a price higher than his or her actual price, allowing the final price to look quite reasonable.

Price Conditioners

These are simply statements, made to make the prospect feel he or she may be in for a higher price than really is the case. For instance, at the prospecting stage the salesperson says: "Gee, the last time I looked they sold for around $_____ ." The figure used is much higher than actual cost. If a prospect balks or starts to walk away, the salesperson says "Don't worry, maybe I can save you some money. Let me ask you this..." Back into a sales presentation.

1. Never use the words "thousand," "hundred," "dollars," "cents," or "and" when quoting price. For example, the price of $1,750.32 is not quoted as one-thousand, seven-hundred fifty

dollars and thirty-two cents. Simply say "Only seventeen-fifty thirty-two". People will know what you mean, but the amount seems a lot less intimidating when quoted this way. Notice the word "only." *Always* add it in front of any prices quoted.

2. Watch your tone of voice and attitude. Act like that's a lot of money and so will your prospect. Act like it's not all that much and so will your prospect.

3. Refer to the cost as an investment.

4. Talk about others costing more before you quote. "You know, similar _____ usually go for $1,500 to $2,000. You're lucky, because of our volume buying I'm happy to tell you the total investment would only be nine ninety five."

This is another price conditioner: The salesperson originally quotes 150 percent to 200 percent more than whatever his or her actual price comes to. By comparison, your price looks a lot cheaper. In addition, the salesperson smiles and acts happy, like he or she is doing the prospect a good turn with such a great price. You can't use all these strategies to create a sense of urgency nor can you use all the price quote strategies on one prospect. What you sell and your personal selling style need to be considered. Select a few strategies you'll feel most comfortable with and memorize them. Have the courage to try them. You'll be amazed at the results.

STEP 10: AVOID WORDS OF REJECTION

Rejection words are words or phases that trigger apprehension or even fear. While this is subtle and many prospects may not be consciously aware of their reaction, it's real. When you use these words you tend to put people on guard. It's easy to avoid this by using the replacement words below:

Eliminate These Words:	*Replace With:*
Cost or price	Total investment
Down payment	Initial investment
Monthly payment	Monthly investment
Contract	Agreement or paperwork

Buy	Own
Sell or sold	Get them involved
Sign (or sign here)	Approve, endorse, or authorize
Pitch (or sales pitch)	Presentation or demonstration
Deal	Opportunity

Add the word "only" in front of any price being quoted. When you are answering an objection or refuting something a prospect says, never use the word "but"; substitute the word "however."

Take the "I" out of your sales interviews. When you use this first-person pronoun, you risk people hearing you say, "I am a smarter, better person." Replace the "I's" with: "you," "my," or "me."

STEP 11: USE TRIAL CLOSES THROUGHOUT YOUR PRESENTATION

A trial close is simply asking the prospect what he or she thinks of something you just said. What you are doing is trying to determine if what you are saying is relevant. Earlier, I said that while you may know 10 or 20 valuable features and benefits about what you sell (I'm hoping that's the case), your prospect is seeing you for only one or two of those at most. The rest mean nothing to the prospect.

That's why, in a good sales presentation, you should be talking about 30 percent of the time, the prospect about 70 percent. If you remember to ask questions of your prospect throughout your sales presentation, the prospect will do more of the talking. One reason some salespeople can't sell is they know too much about what they sell and they feel they must tell it all to each prospect. Don't fall into that trap. Most of what you know about your product or service is actually boring to your prospects.

A good rule to follow is, after you've stated a benefit of what you sell, to ask the prospect if that's why he or she might buy. Here's an example of stating a feature, benefit, and question.

"Mr. _____ , this model has a baked-on, triple coat of weather-proof paint. That means that you won't have to perform any exterior maintenance for the next four years. We guarantee it. Of course, I don't know for sure, but was I correct in understanding that you're replacing the old model because of maintenance problems?"

If the prospect says "Yes," I pull out my warranty to prove the point, in writing. But if he says, "Not really," my response would be, "What is?" I quit talking about the paint finish and warranty. It's a big deal to me, but I'm not the buyer, he is. I need to know what's a big deal to him.

If the prospect should say, "Well, that's one of them," my response would be, "Good, now tell me what else is." By asking questions and qualifying what the prospect is saying, your sales presentation never gets dry and boring. You are continually talking about issues that are of importance to the prospect.

You can't keep using the same phrases to ask questions over and over again. People become uncomfortable when you sound like a memorized speech. Here are three ways to ask questions, with a few examples of each. You need to write out your own questions, in your own words, and rehearse them. When you ask someone how a third party, close to them, might feel about something, the answer is how *he* or *she* feels at the moment. Try the third-party technique on someone who is reluctant to answer your questions. Just remember, only use it once or twice in any interview.

1. *Ask His or Her Opinion.* "What do you think of that?" or "Would that be important to you? " or "Can you use that feature?" or "Is that one of the reasons you're considering _____ ?"

2. *Reverse.* "I don't suppose you'd have much opportunity to use that feature, would you?" or "I guess that's not a really important issue, right?"

3. *Third Party.* "How do you feel your employees would like that?" or "If you showed this to your wife, what do you suppose she'd say?"

7

Closing-the-Sale Strategies

Why do so many salespeople place so much weight on the closing part of the sale? Because it is at this stage where most salespeople have the most difficulty.

There are some things you must understand about closing sales in order to be an effective closer. I should call them secrets because for the most part, few salespeople know or understand them.

Most of the reasons people give you for not buying are smoke, bologna, often lies. There are only a few legitimate reasons a salesperson fails to close a sales presentation. Here are the three you'll hit almost every time.

1. *No Real Need.* They may have a vague interest or curiosity—that's why people will let you give complicated bids, make appointments for long sales interviews, and so on. But without a real need, they'll never buy.

2. *Inability to Afford or Finance Purchase.* Occasionally, people will be financially well off and still feel they can't afford you if their perceived need is low.

3. *They can get the same or what* they perceive *as the same or very similar at a better price or some other advantage.*

When I teach my sales classes on closing, I ask this question: "What's the most frustrating part of selling?"

The answer is, spending all kinds of time, effort, and emotional energy trying to sell someone who acted very interested until you gave your whole story (and price), then suddenly becomes disinterested and won't close no matter what efforts you use.

I then ask the question, "What could possibly be even more frustrating than that?"

The answer, the same situation, except the prospects, trying to avoid feeling guilty for wasting your time, suddenly turn on you. They find fault with you, your company, or your product or service as their excuse. They become cold and distant. They treat you with disdain. They won't take your phone calls. They won't discuss possible reasons and solutions. In a few cases they may become somewhat aggressive or even abusive if you persist. Just about everyone in selling has experienced such situations.

How does that make a salesperson feel? What does it do to his or her self-esteem? I've seen excellent salespeople quit a promising career in selling for this very reason. When this happens over and over again it can really tear a person down. Salespeople can become depressed and disillusioned. Some salespeople will blame it on just bad-luck prospecting. Others may feel the company they represent is at fault. Some feel their product or service is at fault.

The truth is, the salesperson is the only one at fault. The salesperson, no one else. This is a totally avoidable problem; it doesn't have to be this way. After reading this section, you'll see how easy it is to avoid this problem completely.

THE SEVEN STAGES OF THE SALES PROCESS

1. Prospecting
2. Qualifying
3. Presentation
4. Trial closes
5. Objections
6. Closing
7. After sale

Most people believe that the closing process starts at the end of a sales presentation. Wrong! The closing starts immediately, in the prospecting stage.

WHY IS IT SO HARD TO CLOSE SALES?

All prospects have a tendency to procrastinate; it's simply human nature. You do it, I do it, everybody does it. When given a choice, prospects will delay a buying decision. Even when people have a valid need to buy, closing becomes increasingly difficult on:

1. Products or services they know little about

2. Costly items

They feel a sense of confusion. They experience the fear of making a wrong decision. Remember that nobody *wants* to procrastinate. It makes most people very uncomfortable.

This is *why* the salesperson *must* use high pressure to close sales. Now, before you jump up out of your seat and throw this book away, let me explain. This is *not* the old-fashioned kind of high pressure we may see in a movie where the salesperson is beating his or her fist on the desk and shouting. This is more assertive behavior. In order to be effective, this high pressure must be very subtle. Expect people to resist initially. Nobody likes pressure, but I promise you, once you use it and get a commitment from the prospects, they'll be glad also.

The salesperson should be doing 30 percent of the talking and asking enough questions so the prospect speaks about 70 percent of the time. Salespeople who fail to observe that rule and talk too much create another problem. It's called overselling a product or service. What happens is that after they get through presenting their sales talk, they don't ask for an order, but just keep on talking. Why?

The answer is they fear asking somebody to buy. They fear making the prospect upset. They fear ruining a perfectly good rapport they have developed with the prospect. They fear appearing pushy. Most importantly, they fear rejection. They either never ask the prospect to buy or accept the first objection the prospect offers and leave. These salespeople do not earn very much money.

In addition to never closing, there are other problems salespeople create by overselling. They create confusion in the prospect with too much information. People can decide to buy, start to doubt themselves, and finally decide to wait—all while some salesperson is babbling away.

TED'S SALES RULE

Most people don't need, or even want, to know
everything you know about what you sell.

THE RULE OF DIMINISHING RETURNS

The selling process has a flow to it. You build people's interest gradually to a peak as you talk about the benefits of your product or service. It's easiest to get a buying decision while they are at that peak. That's why trial closes are so invaluable. Most prospects don't show any outward signs of peaking.

Think of a clock with a pendulum. Think of your prospect's interest level as that pendulum. As you present selling information it swings in a positive direction. As you continue to talk, the pendulum continues toward positive as the prospect becomes more and more convinced. Eventually the prospect's interest peaks. Unfortunately, there is rarely if ever any outward sign of this. The prospect just sits there, listening, thinking about what you sell and if he or she should or should not buy. Much of this is on a subconscious level, but it's there. If the salesperson does not use the trial closes but just keeps on talking, the process slowly but surely goes into reverse. The prospect is now giving greater weight to the reasons to delay a decision.

Once the process starts to reverse, it becomes difficult to stop, and even more difficult to reverse again. Once people make a buying decision, you need to complete the transaction.

The longer you talk past this peak, the less chance you have of closing the sale. Eventually, people will sell themselves on not buying. *You must use closing techniques.*

Why do people keep talking and not asking closing questions? In nearly every case the answer is fear. Fear the prospect will say no. Fear the prospect will be upset, fear of rejection, and so on—groundless fears that exist only in the salesperson's mind. Fears that allow perfectly good prospects to not buy, simply because no one asked them to do so.

How can you know when to stop giving information and close the sale? By asking questions in the form of trial closes.

WHY SOME PEOPLE HAVE A PROBLEM BEING ASSERTIVE

A lot of reasons are given—a few true, most simply excuses because the truth is too uncomfortable. The truth being, as in the prospecting stage of selling, that some individuals fear being assertive.

It's nothing to be ashamed about. Even sales professionals with years of experience occasionally face this feeling. If you understand why you feel this fear, you can, nearly every time, beat it. There are two reasons this issue may arise. The first dates back to childhood; the second is an issue of low self-esteem.

The first starts out in our childhood, when mom warned us, "Don't talk to strangers!" If you don't believe me, I just want you to close your eyes right now. Think back to childhood. How did you feel then when you'd see a stranger? Case closed!

Again, let me assure you, that was certainly an okay, appropriate behavior when you were a small child. However, as an adult today, it certainly is not.

So first, we all start out in life with that little gem hanging around out necks. The next fear we learn is, don't offend guests. Remember when people were coming over to your house to visit? What did mom and dad warn you about?

Be polite! Don't talk back! Never sass or you'll be punished! How about "God's watching!" The point to this is that nearly every one of us in childhood was warned against doing the very skills that make a good salesperson! Is it any wonder that so many people shiver at the thought of selling for a living?

A lot of people have told me "I just can't be that aggressive!" Let me promise you this: A good sales closer is never aggressive, but he or she is always assertive.

Assertive, Aggressive, or Abusive?

I equate aggressive with abusive and people won't buy from or trust people who abuse them. However, everybody respects people who have enough courage to stand up for what they believe in. That is simply being assertive. I say this now to you with all sincerity:

TED'S SALES RULE

If you don't believe what you sell is of real
benefit to your prospects, find another job
selling what you can believe in!

If you sincerely believe that what you sell is of benefit to your customers, then being assertive is much easier.

Self-esteem

The second issue is self-esteem. If you don't have a good sense of self-esteem you'll have a difficult time being assertive. I discussed this in Chapter 4 on prospecting and I'm repeating it here because it is so closely related to your success as a salesperson.

There are some really excellent audiocassette tapes and books you can buy from bookstores or get from your library to assist you in understanding healthy assertiveness and healthy self-esteem. I strongly suggest anyone in business, most especially sales, study these.

A FIVE-POINT SUCCESS CLOSING PATTERN THAT WILL PUT YOU IN THE TOP 20 PERCENT

1. Build into your sales presentation reasons to buy "now."
2. Don't give sales talks without all the decision makers present.
3. Use trial closes and have at least six memorized.

4. Expect objections and have memorized answers to all common ones.

5. Use closes frequently; don't take no for an answer. Memorize at least six closes.

Step 1—Build In Reasons to Buy Now

This is sometimes known as creating a sense of urgency. Ever go into a store for a closer look at something in the show window, and the salesperson says "Gee, I think we're sold out." Suddenly you feel a sense of loss and you start asking the salesperson to check the stockroom.

A banker might say, "If you're planning to do something today I'd better check the rates to see if they are still that low. Did you want me to go ahead if I can still get you that rate?"

A car salesperson may say, "I don't know if I can sell this one, it's our only one left to show." If the customer says check, the salesperson says, "Should I put a hold on it?"

People always want something they think is in short supply or hard to get.

Another way to create a sense of urgency is to mention casually, early in the sale, that you hope the price you quote will be accepted because you're expecting a price increase any time.

A consultant or other seller of a service can convince prospects that there are certain standards in business dealings he or she will not deviate from. Under certain conditions the seller will not do business, but would rather walk away from potential business. While this must be done in a subtle way or it won't work, in this case the prospect feels honored to do business with you.

Examine what you sell carefully for reasons why someone should buy now and start speaking about these reasons from the very start of the sales process. Point out to a prospect that something will be different later on and this is really the right time to act.

One last technique: A real-estate salesperson could say "I'd love to show you that property, providing somebody hasn't put in an offer on it. It's really a nice property. Let me check."

Step 2—Don't Give a Sales Talk without All the Decision Makers Present

One of the most difficult objections for any salesperson is, "I need to consult with a third party." They never tell you this until they have gotten every question answered and you've quoted your price. The only effective way to stop this from happening will call for a little assertiveness from the salesperson. You have your own rule, which is:

> *Rule: You don't give sales presentations without all the decision makers present, ever!* (That also includes quoting prices.)

When you are making appointments, say something like: "Mr. _____ , be sure to include anyone in the meeting who you think has to be there in order for a decision to be made. I don't care who you invite, attorney, CPA, partner (wife), whoever. I'll be happy to answer any questions any of them may have."

If he says he is the only decision maker, you say, "Great. It's good to meet a person who can make a decision on his own without a committee."

You've just put pressure on the prospect to decide now! Do you think this will lose some appointments for you? Yes it will. What kinds of prospects would be the most offended? If your answer is the ones who would not buy anyway, you're right. Guaranteed. The ones who planned to waste your time. If you think about it, only people who have decided in advance they don't want to buy from you would really be offended.

Step 3—Use Trial Close Questions

A trial close is a question you ask about how the prospect feels about ownership of your product or service. You ask a trial close *each time* you present a new benefit (feature) of your product or service. If the prospect disagrees, you simply continue on. If the prospect *agrees,* you *stop* all selling immediately and *close!*

Why?

Rule: You know too much !!

You know a great many excellent reasons why people should buy your product or service. Actual studies show nearly all prospects have one or, perhaps at the most, two, dominating reasons to buy what you sell. The rest is just idle conversation to them. (Remember the rule of selling: *People don't buy for your reasons, they buy for theirs*.)

Once you get to their reason, you have to close. Otherwise what happens is as you gab on and on, afraid to close, they decide to buy, reconsider, and then decide not to buy—all while you are talking away about things of very little importance to them.

The trial close is designed to see where the prospect is in the sales process. Start asking him or her about halfway through the sales presentation. You need to memorize at least half a dozen trial closes, such as:

> "It comes in red, green, and orange. Which color do you think you'd pick?"
>
> "I think we *may* have one left. I'm not sure. Should I check?"
>
> "What do you think the neighbors would say if you drove home in this model?"
>
> "How soon do you need this?"
>
> "When would you start using the computer?"
>
> "What would your partner (wife) say?"
>
> "How would you feel taking that home today?"

When you get a negative response, find out why and continue selling on that particular issue.

If you get a positive response, *stop everything* and start a close, *immediately*!

Step 4—Expect Objections and Have Memorized Answers to All Common Ones

I'm amazed at how prospects' objections can cause salespeople so much distress. The more experienced salespeople, the 20-percent salespeople, not only expect objections but they worry if they don't hear any.

If you study human behavior, one thing you'll learn is that when people decide to buy something, they have big fights with themselves! As you are selling prospects, their minds are racing to decide, "Should I or shouldn't I?" They are thinking about all the reasons why they should buy. They also are thinking about all the reasons why they should *not* buy.

Those are the objections you hear. They are really thinking out loud. At that point, most people only half believe the objection themselves. They verbalize what's on their minds so you can either validate it or show them why it doesn't apply.

This validation issue is tricky. If a prospect raises an objection and you get a look on your face like you've just been beaten, that's it. Case closed. Even if your words are positive, your expression says to the prospect, "You're right, I'm wrong." On a subconscious level, the prospect immediately sees that he or she was right not to buy and the objection can become cast in stone. Bingo, another sale down the tubes.

I keep repeating all this assertive stuff for a very important reason. When prospects raise objections, not only does your answer need to be delivered in an assertive fashion, but also your facial expressions, voice inflection, and body language must show your total conviction that what you are suggesting they buy is a good, positive decision for them to make. You must believe also.

That's why I suggest that if you truly can't believe in what you sell, you are not going to be enough of an actor to pull this off, time after time. Remember, when the objection is first raised, they are not at all sure, even if they talk as if they are. Your answer, delivered with positive conviction and honest belief, can often mean the difference in making a sale.

As with any other part of the selling process, you must know in advance what you are going to say. To make a sales call and simply respond to emotions of statements of the moment is sales suicide. I know many salespeople who do just that. I told you before, salespeople are divided into two groups: the 80 percent and the 20 percent.

The time to think of an answer to an objection is never in front of a prospect. Do it when you have time to think calmly of all the valid reasons the prospect should buy.

The Three Kinds of Objections

There are three and only three kinds of objections. Learn these and you'll never feel lost again when objections are raised.

1. Real objection (about something specific)

   Example: "I don't like the color," or "I'm short of cash."

2. Hidden objection (this is an unspoken one, camouflaged by numerous false objections)

   Example: A person may be embarrassed to admit not being able to afford your product or service, and therefore raises a series of false objections.

3. False objection (vague, nothing specific)

   Example: "I want to think it over" or "I don't believe in buying on the first sales call."

How You Can Spot a Hidden Objection

1. You know you're getting a false objection when somebody continues to resist after you've given sound reasons why his or her objection is not valid.

2. Each time you answer one objection, you get another objection. For instance, someone says, "I won't have that much money until next month, my bank account is too low." You then suggest you can put it on a credit card and he or she says, "I don't want to pay interest on top of this price." You suggest that since the money will be available next month, the credit card can be paid off in 30 days without interest. The person then tells you that he or she doesn't know where the credit card is. It's like trying to step on Jell-O. It just keeps rolling around all over the place. When you pursue a prospect like this it can also possibly result in an argument.

Why Do People Do This?

The true reason is too embarrassing for them to state. Often they feel they can't afford your product or service. They may really not have the money. Maybe their credit rating is horrible. Perhaps they lied to you about being a true prospect and have no real need; they were simply curious. Maybe they are not the real decision maker and lied about that. It may be that they have seen other salespeople and have gotten a lower price. It could be they have already purchased from your competitor and are interviewing you just to see if they missed anything.

This is why qualifying up front, at the prospecting stage, is so critical to your success. Most times the qualification process will weed out these kinds of prospects before you spend a lot of frustrating time trying to sell people, who, for reasons only they know, *can't* be sold. The salesperson must have the courage to insist on hard answers at the prospecting stage.

It is true: When you don't qualify prospects you certainly get a lot more sales presentations to give. You also get an awful lot of people who take up a lot of your time and then never buy.

How Do You Handle a False Objection?

When a prospect raises an objection, don't be quick with a response. Often, the first few objections are raised to camouflage the real or hidden objection:

Before you answer, qualify. "Mary, let me ask you this. Is that the only reason you wouldn't want to go ahead today?" or "Besides that, is there any other reason that would prevent you from going ahead right now?"

You may get two or three responses. Each time qualify *what else* would hold the prospect back. Always be specific. The question is about buying now. You must be as specific as he or she is vague. Remember, don't actually answer the false objections or you'll provide ammunition for additional ones. Don't answer the vague objection but just say, "Besides that, is there any other reason?" The prospect will feel as if you had answered the objection.

Usually the last one will be the real objection. You'll recognize it because it will not be a vague one, but will be about something specific such as price, delivery, and so on.

Ignore the false objectives and deal with the specific. Then go to a close.

If you try the above techniques and still can't get a specific objection, confront the prospect like this:

"Jack, I have a strong suspicion there's something you're not telling me—something that's keeping you from making a decision. I want you to tell me what it is."

Examples of Dealing with False Objections to Find the Hidden One

1. Ask questions that project your prospect into the future:

   "If I could _____ , would you be prepared to go ahead with this today?"

2. Qualify stated objections:

   "Is that the only reason, Mr. _____ ?"
   "Assuming we could deal with that right now, is there anything else that would stop you from going ahead with this now?"
   "What else . . .?"

3. Close after each objection:

   Prospect: "I can't afford it."
   You: "As I understand you, you are saying this is too much money at one time. Am I correct?"
   Prospect: "Yes."
   You: "So if I can show you a way to own this right away, but pay for it over a period of time, you'd want to go ahead now, correct?"
   Prospect: "Well, no, not really."
   You (acting slightly surprised): "Oh, money isn't the only issue then, is it?"
   Prospect: "Well, no."
   You: "What is?"
   Remember: You can't sell as long as an objection remains unspoken. You must bring it out in the open. Do this by gentle probing with questions. Don't allow prospects to lie to you.

Eight Magic Rules for Handling All Objections

1. Don't fear objections. Fear when you get none. It's a sign the prospect has little or *no* interest. In this case, when prospects just listen, ask them lots of open questions.

2. Don't become an adversary. See objections as requests for more information.

3. Listen carefully to the exact words and tone used by the prospect.

4. Restate what you think you heard the prospect say. "As I understand it, Bill, you're saying the price is too high. Do I have that correct?"

5. Let the prospect respond. Listen carefully. Sometimes you will not have understood the objection correctly. Other times the prospect will answer his or her own objection, such as:

   "I guess when you think about how everything else goes up in price, it's probably okay. I haven't bought these for a long time."

   If a prospect backs off, *don't continue with an answer anyway.* Ignore and continue as if it never happened.

6. If the prospect agrees it is an objection, then do give an answer.

7. Never give clues you have memorized the answer. Speak slowly as if you just thought of the answer.

8. *Don't ever ask if they accept your answer.* ("Does that clear it up?" or "Okay?" or "Can we agree on that?" or "Does that answer your question?") People will follow your lead. Act confident as if your answer was the final word. Just go to a trial close. *Assume* they accept your answer. *Assume* they will buy now. To do any differentiy gives credibility to their objection and can turn a molehill into a huge mountain.

During your sales presentation you need to be aware that before you attempt any close, you should reduce their choices to two or, at the most, three. People get very confused with more than three choices.

Three Tough, Specific Objections and Answers

"I Have a Friend in the Business"

If they really do have a friend in the business, here are some very valid reasons for not doing business with those people. Keep in mind that most people want to do what's best for them, not to lose by giving some friend business. Remind people it's hard to complain to friends about delivery, service, and quality. Also remind them friends might get mad if they ask for a better deal. Remember the old adage "The quickest way to lose a friend is to have money dealings with him or her."

Sometimes you might act pleasantly surprised and say, "Gee, that's great, who is it?" Watch the prospect's face when you do this. If he or she looks surprised or flustered, chances are this is a bluff and simply a stall to get rid of you. If the person acts cagey about revealing the name you could say, "Gee, almost everyone in my field knows almost everyone else. There are no hard feelings. What reason might you have for keeping the person's name a secret?"

If he or she still declines, treat it as a hidden objection by going back to, "Besides that, is there any other reason you wouldn't want to go ahead today?"

"Your Price Is Too High"

Compared to what? If prospects have been shopping and can give you a specific example, then it's a real objection. If, on the other hand, they have no idea what your product or services are worth and say that, it's a sign of low interest. You have not convinced them and they wouldn't buy at any price. You need to get back into your sales presentation. You must prove to them that by buying, they are getting value received.

"I Want to Think It Over" ("Call Me Back for a Decision")

You say: "Sorry, I don't make callbacks."

Explain to your prospect: "The reason is, it's in your best interest to make a decision now. I've just reviewed why you should buy now. This is the right time to make the decision, now, while the information is still fresh in your mind."

"I know you're a busy person with a lot of things going on in your life. By tomorrow, chances are you won't remember all the details. As time passes it will be even more difficult to make such a decision. If I let you procrastinate I wouldn't be doing my job. I'd really be doing you a disservice. I'm a professional and I want to do what's right for you."

On the surface this response seems to take a great deal of courage, yet if you review the last 20 times people brushed you off with the "I want to think it over" response, I'd almost bet you never sold any of them when you called them back. In fact, I'd almost bet that when you called back, some of them wouldn't even come to the phone.

In nearly every case when you hear this response the prospect has decided not to buy, usually for an unspoken (hidden) reason and is seeking a way to get rid of you. By standing your ground you can often get to the real reason for the no sale. Actually, you have almost nothing to lose by using this tactic.

Step 5—The Close

A lot of salespeople put great faith in having a clever close strategy. I don't. I truly believe that your real sales close is done early on, when you ask the qualification questions. Each step must be properly completed before you proceed to the next. I think the close is simply the natural cumulation of a well-done sales interview.

The truth is that if you sell a product or service someone has a valid need for and you can clearly demonstrate that to this person, there really is very little resistance to your request for an order. The closing strategy I use most frequently is to just ask for the order. It works more often than not *if* I've done everything else properly.

Another truth in selling is that it's a numbers game. That is, no matter how well you qualify, present, and close, you can only sell a certain percentage. No one sells everyone. I've failed with prospects I would have bet a month's wages would buy. I've sold people I originally thought were time wasters. Do your very best at all times, but have the courage to know when to quit and move on to someone else. That's another mark of the successful salesperson.

Selling, when you do it right, by the book, is a very simple business. It's also a very hard business, especially the prospecting and closing parts. Yet time after time salespeople get tangled up in all sorts of complications they create for themselves. They then become depressed and start to doubt their abilities and their sales drop to just below their shoe tops.

Why? Simply because they try to take shortcuts. They change what they do to save time or because they become lazy. Perhaps they have low self-esteem and they fear the assertive part of selling, so they drop that part out. Maybe they back off when a prospect gets a little gruff about answering qualification questions.

Remember this if nothing else from my book: When you hit a sales slump, stop. Pull out this book and reread it as if you've never seen it before. When you see areas you have reinvented, don't make excuses. Just go back to doing it by the book. I promise you, these strategies work, but only if you do them properly.

Over the years I have worked side by side with, managed, and trained more salespeople than I can possibly remember or count. Chapter 8 discusses excellent closing strategies I've seen used and personally used myself, all with great success. No one would consider memorizing them all. I'd suggest you become comfortable with a few at a time.

A Warning on Closing

Use soft words such as paperwork, never contract; "just authorize here" or "I'll need your okay here," never "sign here"; investment or initial investment or monthly investment, never money, down payment, or monthly payment.

8

Closing Strategies to Put Money in Your Bank Account

ASKING FOR THE ORDER

There's nothing tricky about this close. It's very honest and straight-forward. You just ask the prospect if he or she is ready to go ahead. If you ever get nervous during a closing pattern and can't remember a closing strategy, you can always fall back and use this one. You might be surprised to know how many millions of dollars in goods and services are sold every year by people using this close alone.

"Should I write that up?"

"Is this the model you want me to have delivered?"

"Are you ready to go ahead then?"

THE TRIAL-ORDER CLOSE

In some selling situations a buyer may hesitate because you are an unknown source and he or she is not sure about you. In this event, instead of forcing the issue and getting a rejection, you can offer to do a little business with the buyer to prove your ability. A serious prospect with a valid reason to hesitate will tend to take advantage of such an offer.

"Look, I understand you're using XYZ Company. Having a second source in the event something goes wrong could be very important. Why not try a trial order from me today to see if everything I told you was true. This is the best time to try out a second source of supply, when everything is going well, not when you have a crisis. Make sense?"

THE CHOICE

Here you offer a choice. No matter which the prospect selects, he or she has purchased.

"Which color do you prefer, red or green?"

"How do you want that shipped? Regular UPS Ground or UPS Overnight Air?"

"Do you want the full-year membership with the 20 percent savings or the six-month trial?"

THE PUPPY-DOG CLOSE I

So named because it's been used by pet stores for years. You allow the prospect to obtain possession of your product or use your service for a short time. Office-machine companies frequently use this method. The idea is that once someone has possession of something desirable it becomes very hard to part with it.

I would not recommend a very long trial because the products can become damaged if you take them back. You also find a few sharpies who will take advantage, so be sure they sign a written agreement that it's your property to pick up and that they are financially responsible for any damage. In the case of products that use replaceable supplies, such as paper and toner for copy machines, it's best to put in writing who pays for such items.

THE PUPPY-DOG CLOSE II

Some companies offer a free trial as in the above. However, to better protect themselves and also to be better assured that the trial will result in a sale, they change the strategy a little. They start out the same, offering a prospect a free trial for, say, two weeks. Only after the prospect agrees does he or she find out the company writes it up as a sale, with a very generous return privilege for the agreed period.

The difference is this: They complete all financing arrangements (they know the prospect has credit before delivery of anything) and the prospect signs a purchase agreement. If the prospect doesn't exercise his or her right to return the product during the trial period, he or she owns a new product.

Of course, some people get upset and complain when they find out the free trial requires a purchase commitment. Yet if a person or firm is serious about purchasing, this is usually not a deal stopper, so long as there is a clearly written agreement to return the product without penalty. It does burn off the people who might see an ad or direct-mail piece and decide to take advantage of a freebie with no intent to buy.

THE FOLLOW-THE-LEADER CLOSE

If your company has any famous or well-known clients, try to get letters of recommendation, or at least information on what they purchased. Use this when people balk at closing. It's amazing how people will follow when they think someone important and/or famous is a fellow user.

THE "YOU DON'T QUALIFY" CLOSE

When you offer a choice to a prospect, instead of trying to sell the top of the line as the prospect expects, say something such as: "Perhaps you should consider the middle unit. You may not be ready for the top model just yet." Many people will consider that a challenge and buy the larger one to "show you."

THE "YOU BEAT ME, I'M LEAVING" CLOSE

Remember the discussion about prospects with hidden objections? I know a salesman who will stand up, put his coat on, close up his briefcase, and say to the prospect. "Well, I guess it's finished, wouldn't you say?"

The prospect will start to relax because he or she feels victorious and says, "Yes."

Salesperson: "Can I just ask you one last question?"

Prospect: "Sure, what is it?"

Salesperson: "What was it I said or did that made you decide not to buy?"

In most cases, with defenses down, the prospect will give an honest answer. My salesperson friend will then start in all over again with the presentation to cover the problem just mentioned by the prospect.

THE NO-SECRET CLOSE

"Look, it's not a secret. I want your business. Tell me, how can I do that?"

This is especially effective when you have been attempting unsuccessfully to close several times. Many salespeople avoid it because the prospect may say there is no way. My feeling is that if that's the case, you are better off putting all cards on the table. There is nothing more demoralizing than chasing a hopeless prospect. In reality I've found most people at this point will bring out some hidden objection you were not familiar with, thus giving you an additional opportunity to close.

THE PROBLEM-SOLVING CLOSE

"Mr. Jones, I came into your office an hour ago because you had a problem."

"Now you seem to have a second problem, because you have to get rid of me. Of course you can do that by simply asking me to leave and if you do, I'll certainly leave. Truthfully, though, that won't solve your original problem, will it? Bill, I'd like to suggest we spend a few additional minutes together and see if we can't solve that problem also. Make sense?"

THE YES CLOSE

Ask a series of questions that will get a yes response, finishing with a closing question.

"This is the color you liked, right?"

"You liked our long-term warranty, right?"

"You did say our price fits your budget, correct?"

"You checked our reputation out with the Better Business Bureau, correct?"

"We should get this ordered now, while they are still available, right?"

THE ASSUMPTIVE CLOSE

In an assumptive close, by using positive body language, actions, and words, you act as if the order were already given and that the sales presentation is simply a formality to clear up minor details. For instance, you get your order pad out early in the presentation and during the sales presentation, as you get details settled such as price, which model, and so on, you write them down on the order blank, in front of the prospect.

During the presentation you never use tentative words, only positive. "If" becomes "when." "If you decide to go ahead" becomes "When I deliver this I'm sure your wife will be thrilled to start using it" or "Did you say Tuesday was a good delivery day?"

You then simply hand the completed order form to the prospect and say, "Just okay this and we'll have it for you on Tuesday, the day you mentioned was good."

THE "IF YOU WERE ME" CLOSE

This is another way to locate hidden objections. In this case you are actually asking the prospect how he or she wants to be sold.

You: "Can I ask your opinion of something that's important to me?"

Prospect: "Sure."

You: "If you were sitting here in my chair, what would you have to do, or say, in order to sell you?"

THE PROSPECTS-OPINION CLOSE

Another way to effectively use this technique is when a prospect raises some objection that you are not sure about. Instead of offering a concession when such an objection is voiced, ask:

"Tell me Jack, if you were me, what would you feel would be a fair solution to that issue for both of us?"

You've flattered the prospect by asking for his opinion and you've also put the prospect on his best honor, asking for something "Fair" to both of you. More often than not the prospect will either back off any change or suggest something much less than you might be willing to give.

If the demand is unreasonable, you have made no promise to accept and can continue the negotiation. If, by some slim chance, the demand is really ridiculous, then you may have misjudged the prospect. You might need to save any further time loss and go to the next one.

THE DOLLARS-AND-GOOD-SENSE CLOSE

Find out from the prospect the consequences of not going ahead. Reduce it to dollars. Using a big notepad, draw a line down the middle. On one side write down the cost of your product or service. On the other side write down, one by one, the cost to the prospect of not buying *today*. *Don't* invent the amounts of money. Ask your prospect for his or her best estimate. Never do this without practicing alone first. You *must know in advance* approximately what the figures will be. If you're not reasonably accurate, or if the figures don't add up in your favor, it won't work.

THE BEN FRANKLIN CLOSE

This is just like the Dollars-and-Good-Sense Close, but you list all the reasons (benefits) for the prospect's going ahead *today* versus reasons not to buy. Have the prospect do the writing—it helps to smoke out unspoken (hidden) objections. Again, this requires practice. When you write a benefit, get wordy. Reduce objections to one or two words.

THE SHAME CLOSE

Here you shame someone into buying. Not suggested for sophisticated buyers. Most frequently used by in-home salespeople.

"Doesn't your lovely family deserve this protection?"

"Isn't your peace of mind important enough to go ahead with this today?"

"Isn't the well-being of your children worth a few extra dollars a month?"

THE NO-TIME-LEFT CLOSE

You refer to a shortage (people always want what's hard to get), price increase, or some other reason a quick decision is needed.

"This is the only one left. If you want it I'll need to know now."

"Someone else called about this also. If you don't act now it may be gone when you come back."

"After today I can't write any more orders at this price. Better act now."

If someone asks about a product you can set up a close by saying: "Gee, I think we just sold the last one, they move pretty fast. Let me check. If I do have one should I hold it for you?"

THE "BIG MISTAKE NOT TO BUY" CLOSE

Here you deal with the consequences of not buying. You do that by determining any financial advantage to buying your product or service. For instance, an office-machine salesperson might establish some dollar loss for not using the latest equipment. A burglar-alarm salesperson could show higher insurance costs and also project costs of future burglaries.

"Mr. Prospect, here's the total investment for _____ . It's really a small amount, because if you choose not to invest _____ ."

By making a direct comparison, you have made your price look like a bargain.

THE PRICE-BREAKDOWN CLOSE

This has been used with great success by many salespeople. When something is expensive, break the price down into smaller units. For instance, an insurance salesperson might toss two or three packs of chewing gum on a prospect's table and say, "For the cost of this gum each day you can give your wife and children protection. That's sure worth the price of a few packs of chewing gum isn't it?"

A salesperson, selling a security-alarm system for $2,500 and financeable for three years might quote a price like this: "If you go ahead tonight, we can protect your home and family from the dangers of fire and burglary for less than $2.30 a day."

Per day, per week, per month, per usage are ways to quote prices and make them sound quite reasonable.

THE SMALL-DETAILS CLOSE

Instead of asking for an order directly, you start asking questions about the details.

"Did you say Tuesdays and Thursdays are best for delivery?"

"Do you think the large unit will fit in your office?"

"This is what you were looking for, right?"

"What do you think the neighbors will say when you drive home in this tonight?"

THE REVERSE-QUESTION CLOSE

"You don't mind depriving your family of the pleasure this will bring them?"

"You're probably not interested getting a discount on your next purchase, are you?"

"I suppose your boss wouldn't be too interested if this deal went sour because you used the wrong vendor, right?"

"I guess the money-back guarantee isn't very important, is it?"

THE MISTAKEN ORDER

Make a close on something higher than what the prospect is intending to buy. When the prospect corrects you, agree and write the order on the correction.

"Let's see, you wanted a gross delivered, right?" (to someone looking for a few dozen).

"Tell me, did you want the middle model or the bigger deluxe version for a few thousand more?" (to someone looking for a cheaper, low-end model).

THE COMPROMISE CLOSE

This is another reason to always try to sell top of the line. When the close comes and price objections start flying, you have a way to look good without cutting commission. You don't cut price. What you do is to reduce price by offering a lower product or service.

"I can understand your financial situation, Mr. _____ . However, I'm sure we can agree that you really need _____ .I have a great idea that will allow you to enjoy _____ but at a much lower cost."

THE PROJECTING-INTO-THE-FUTURE CLOSE

This is really a very powerful close. It's one of my favorites because you can use it to answer an objection without promising to concede. It works well when you suspect the prospect may have a hidden objection. When a prospect objects about price, delivery, and so on, don't promise to get him or her a better deal. Instead, ask if you could correct that problem now, would he or she be ready to go ahead now?

"Jack, I hear what you are saying about _____ . If I could get you a better deal on _____ that would be satisfactory, would you be prepared to go ahead today?"

If the prospect says yes, then you have a valid objection, which you now must handle and immediately go for a close. In a lot of cases he or she will hesitate or get evasive by saying "Well, it depends on the price."

You answer: "I understand what you are saying. Assuming the price is okay, would you be ready to go ahead today?"

If the prospect brings up a second reason not to buy today, then do the same thing. "Assuming I can get you an acceptable price and also take care of _____ , would you be ready to go ahead now?" (Always emphasize the words "go ahead now.")

In the event the answer is not on something specific such as price, delivery, terms, and so on, but rather general such as: "I'd like to sleep on it" or "I'll need some time to think it over" or "I never buy on the spot from salespeople," the prospect is not being honest with you.

Don't waste time answering the objection but rather ask questions about why he or she is delaying.

THE INCREASE-SALE CLOSE

This is a close upon a close. When you get a positive response to your closing question, instead of offering to write it up you try to increase the order. Say something like this:

"These will never be on sale at this price again. Why not take an extra while you're here?"

"These make excellent gifts. Why not get a few more for people on your gift list and save time shopping later on?"

"Did I show you the optional _____ ? It's also on sale."

"Great decision. It entitles you to get a 20 percent discount on a second one purchased at the same time."

DO YOU KNOW WHAT BUYER'S REMORSE IS?

You spend hours closing a prospect. You get back to the office to find he or she called and *canceled*! You try to call the prospect back and he or she won't take your call. It's every salesperson's nightmare.

Nine Tested Steps to Prevent Buyer's Remorse

1. Be very careful about how you react when a customer decides to buy from you. Maintain a professional demeanor and act as if that was the only decision you expected and that you do this all the time.

   Never allow yourself to get animated or excited. Don't start saying things such as, "Great! I promise you won't regret your decision" or "I can't thank you enough" or "I'm really thrilled you've decided to go ahead." Don't grab the customer's hand and shake it with lots of enthusiasm. Don't call someone from the new customer's premises to announce that you've made a sale.

   Why? First, you look like a rank amateur and people don't like spending their hard-earned money with amateurs. Second, and worst of all, your excitement tells them you just made a big score, and at their expense. It immediately causes suspicion that they just got taken in some way.

   Know how I thank someone for their business? I actually don't; I just tell the person that a very smart decision was made. After everything else is done, on the way out the door I shake the person's hand, look him or her in the eye, and simply say, "I'm glad you've decided to join our family of satisfied customers. Now you'll have a firsthand opportunity to see why we've been so successful."

2. After you've closed someone and finished all the necessary paperwork, take time to reassure the customer of the wisdom of his or her decision. Paint a little word picture about the pleasure he or she will derive from making this decision.

3. Ask the customer for the reasons he or she bought from you and not a competitor. Don't talk, just listen. As your new customer goes on, he or she is really being sold all over again, out loud. It would be very rare indeed for someone to cancel after that exercise (unless you violate Rule 7, below).

4. Get the product delivered or service started as quickly as possible, even if only a small portion.

5. Get a valid contract properly signed, with all the details in writing. Make sure you are dealing with a person who has the authority to commit to your offer.

6. Getting some money down (or a valid, signed purchase order) is always an excellent binder.

7. Follow up on all promises and details. Any salesperson who violates this rule deserves the consequences.

8. If bad news arises regarding the order, you should be the one to deliver it. While a customer may yip at bad news, he or she will also respect you for your truthfulness and follow-through. This, more than any other factor, is the key to repeat business and referrals.

9. Don't hang around after a sale to socialize, no matter how enticing the offer. It's a big mistake to mix business and social friendship together. Once you've tied up the loose ends, GO!

Develop a sincere reputation as a man or woman of your word. You'll make lifelong business friends, lifelong customers, and lifelong referral sources.

THE ART OF GETTING SALES REFERRALS

I reviewed some of these techniques in an earlier chapter, but since the end of a successful sale is the best time to get sales referrals from a customer, let me show you some methods that really produce.

Getting referrals is beyond a doubt the most common method taught new salespeople as a means of lead procurement. Everyone agrees it's an excellent source of business. Talk to veteran salespeople and they'll assure you they ask for referrals every time.

Now walk up to any salesperson in your organization and ask to see a list of prospects, just the referrals please. Oops! Can't seem to find 'em? Perhaps he or she: (a) left it at home, (b) left it in the car, (c) ran out of paper and used it for the office football pool.

The truth is, this is one of those situations where everyone agrees it's a great idea. Unfortunately, most lack the skills to obtain referrals on a regular basis, feel some rejection because of that, and wind up using other lead-procurement methods. Most salespeople ask "Do you happen to know anyone who wants to buy———?" Of course they usually don't, so the salespeople decide it's just not working and quit. Following are a few tested methods that have worked well for some of the most successful salespeople I've known.

1. The Common Denominator

When I train salespeople on sales-development programs, I identify the common denominators that make a good prospect for that business. I then turn them into what are often called memory joggers or trigger questions. For instance, when selling home-security systems, new home owners are good prospects as are new parents and also people who have had a recent crime problem.

I trained salespeople to ask (after closing and completing the sale) these questions:

"Who do you know who recently moved?"

"Do you have any friends or relatives who just became parents?"

"Anyone you know had a recent crime problem?"

For a company selling car phones, salespeople and people on the go are two categories of good prospects. We had salespeople ask "How many of your friends are in sales?" and "Tell me who this describes: a friend of yours who is always on the go and never at home when you call?"

While most people don't know anyone who wants to buy anything, they know lots of people. A salesperson has to ask in terms people can relate to in order to get the memory flowing.

2. The Address Book

Once in a while people can't think of prospects for you even with the memory jogger or trigger questions. After some blank stares in response to his or her questions, the salesperson can ask "Fred, where do you keep telephone numbers for reference? An address book? Could you get it please?" Let the prospect thumb the book completely for each trigger question.

3. The Reward

Often companies and salespeople will offer a reward for a prospect name that becomes a buyer. This is okay providing the reward is not excessive. Remember, most people you are doing this with have just signed up. Offering some extravagant reward looks like you must be making big bucks on the sale. They start wondering if they just paid too much. If you can, make the reward something connected to your business—an extended warranty, a free service contract, an additional product, and so on. Alarm and phone companies can use a period of free monthly service for each new client obtained.

9

Telemarketing for Success

TELEMARKETING PROS AND CONS

As a sales and marketing consultant, I've had many people call me for advice on how to develop a telemarketing operation for their business. Let's take a look at some of the pros and cons of telemarketing.

Telemarketing is effectively used in these business areas with great success:

1. Lead procurement for salespeople
2. Order taking for companies that advertise through catalogs, direct mail, and in various media (usually an 800 phone number)
3. Customer-service operations
4. Marketing research
5. Political election activities
6. Fund raising

Selling products and services via telephone is where it gets questionable. Usually, developing leads for your sales staff works well if you have the right script and the right people. All you need do is locate prospects who have some degree of interest and let a live salesperson take over. It's when you ask someone for a money decision over the phone that a much higher degree of resistance takes place. The items sold best are usually low cost (i.e., low risk for the consumer to make a decision on).

119

Telemarketing sales talks and answers to common questions must be scripted. Professionally written ones will achieve maximum results.

As with so many industries, computer technology has enhanced the telemarketing industry. There are computer programs that allow a one-person business to telemarket effectively from a personal computer and telephone modem. There are larger systems that allow dozens of telemarketers to work from a single database.

One item used in telemarketing, the automatic dialer that gives a recorded message, is questionable. While I have heard reports of success using it, in some areas of the country numerous complaints have been made to authorities concerning its use. As a businessperson, I would feel such bad press would quickly cancel out any benefits to be gained using it.

Computer technology has also spawned a large number of professional telemarketing operations that you can hire. Some specialize in in-bound calls, such as providing an 800 phone number that they own and on which you can advertise. They take the calls for you. Others concentrate on out-bound calls. They will do your telemarketing for you.

If it sounds really simple, don't believe it. As in all industries, these operations have good and bad operators. Even the best of them won't do as good a job as an in-house system will. Before I'd hire any outside firm, I'd want to speak to at least three business firms to whom they provide the same type of service as what I want. If the telemarketing firm stalls or acts like that's a problem, you can bet that hiring them will be a more serious problem.

Problem Areas to Be Aware Of

1. The common use of voice mail makes telemarketing to business firms much more complicated.

2. Using existing outside salespeople and other employees rarely works. Hiring people who are specifically right for telemarketing is somewhat different from hiring the other persons on your staff.

3. It can get expensive fast, especially if your initial plan is flawed.

Reasons to Use Telemarketing

Some of the big reasons telemarketing is so hot right now:

1. Prospecting is much easier and time spent on the telephone much more effective.

2. With advertisements and direct mail, you must be careful to anticipate and answer potential objections or the reader simply discards your offer. With telemarketing you can answer questions for customers and prospects on the spot.

3. Compared to direct selling efforts, telemarketing is very cost effective, especially with the newer computer software programs.

4. Results can be easily measured.

USING TELEMARKETING AS A SALES APPOINTMENT TOOL

As you have seen in the earlier chapters, selling gets involved very quickly. The hardest part of selling is the prospecting stage. I believe that properly applied telemarketing strategies can be a big benefit to the small businessperson who will be relying on direct sales. Since you are calling on the telephone and not in person for the initial contact, qualifying prospects by telephone gets tricky.

When you call someone for an in-person appointment you can't really start a big qualification process. You just lose too many. These kinds of telemarketing calls, to be a success, are very short in nature and much of the qualification must be done when you arrive for the appointment.

HOW TO MAKE TELEMARKETING A BIG WINNER FOR YOU

Before you get into the actual techniques of telemarketing, it's important you fully understand the concept of telemarketing. Many people just starting out have no concept of what it takes to telemarket successfully. I've seen many salespeople who considered themselves a failure when in fact they were doing well above average and would have been considered a success by anyone else's standards.

Here's an example from my own sales career when I was in the security-alarm industry:

I needed to develop at least one new appointment a day, five days a week. In order to do that I would make 20 cold telemarketing calls a day from my office, each and every morning. I found my success rate at reaching businesspeople was greatest between 8:00 A.M. and 10:00 A.M. Out of the 100 dials I would average 47 decision makers I could actually get on the telephone. Out of the 47 I reached, 13 would set appointments, one of which would cancel out in some way. Out of the 12 appointments a week I would make, two of those would become customers. Here's how my own activities broke down:

100 cold calls = 47 people reached

47 decision makers reached = 13 appointments

13 appointments = 1 cancellation

12 completed appointments = 2 sales

The rejection factor is very high no matter how successful you may be. It does not take a math genius to see that I couldn't even reach one half of the people I called, and for every yes I got to my request for an appointment, I got a lot of nos. I must also tell you that at that time voice-mail systems were not as common in business as they are today. Today, with voice mail so commonplace, I doubt I would reach more than 30 or 35 decision makers out of 100 calls instead of the 47 I used to.

I don't know how important two new sales a week would mean to you in your selling. To me it made the difference in my career. I was top salesperson in the company and became sales manager after two years.

A TELEMARKETER'S STRATEGY

I learned a trick from another salesperson that was very helpful in handling all that rejection. Never count the yeses, just count the nos. Every time someone would reject my offer, I'd just put down a hash mark and continue on. I knew the more nos I collected, the closer to a sale I was getting.

TELEMARKETER'S CREDO

Make
it
happen!

---

18 Rules for Successful Telemarketing

This telemarketing system will help you achieve great results in your sales efforts. In effect, it is simply a time-tested system that will give you a proven formula to allow you to reach your goals

Almost without exception, successful salespeople in all types of sales attribute a great deal of their success to the development of good telephone techniques and habits. Let me share some important points to remember when you use the telephone. The following information is basic to all telemarketing. Please read it carefully, as many times as necessary, until you fully understand it.

1. Watch your voice speed and tone. The only way a prospect might know you are unsure or frightened using the phone is your voice. Speaking rapidly sounds to many like high pressure. Hesitating and hemming and hawing sounds like someone who doesn't know what he or she is doing. Speak just as you do to people in person. The best way to learn this is to tape-record your calls and listen to them. You'll be surprised at what you hear and also surprised at how easy it is to correct your technique.

2. Reach the right person. You can't sell secretaries or receptionists—they don't have the authority to buy, so why burn time trying to sell them?

3. Set aside a regular time each day. Decide in advance how many people you will talk to before quitting and don't stop dialing until you reach your goal. Only the actual prospects you speak

to should be counted. No-answers, busy lines, or people not in don't count. You'll be surprised at how many calls you must make just to speak to a live prospect.

4. Telemarketing is strictly a numbers game. You can't succeed without constantly working at it. Be mentally prepared for and expect rejection, but don't take it personally. These rejections are against whatever you are calling about, not against you.

5. Usually you'll need to spend at least two to four uninterrupted hours per session to get good results. If you are going to do telemarketing, ultimately it will be necessary for you to make a short-range commitment to doing it on a regular basis. Making a few random phone calls between other duties is not telemarketing, it's called fooling yourself.

6. Have all your prospects' names in front of you before starting. When practical, group calls by area if you are setting appointments to save on travel time. Work from a quiet place with all your supplies and information at your fingertips. Noise in the background, such as TV or radios, kids playing, people talking, and so on, is distracting to both you and the people you call. They mark you as an amateur.

7. Follow a written script. Have written answers in front of you for common objections and expect them. Never telemarket from memory. Sometimes a prospect will ask an unexpected question or make an unusual remark you don't expect. It's easy to forget or fumble your words. Telemarketing moves fast when you have a good prospect on the phone and you can lose this prospect with just a few wrong words. Always be prepared.

8. Pause between calls only to make brief notes on your cards, then go immediately to the next call. Sometimes a difficult person will make your work just a little less fun by giving you a hard time. Don't let anyone control your feelings. Don't stop to think about a difficult situation. Go quickly to your next call and keep your goals clearly in mind.

9. Always speak with a smile. There's something positive that happens to the speaking quality of your voice when you smile. A lot of people you call will react much more positively. Try it!

10. Be assumptive, expect to get a yes. When closing, give prospects a choice. You need to have written out several closes. You try one, the prospect objects, you answer the objection, and finish with another close. Sometimes you'll go through several. It's important to be persistent. Don't hang up until you've had several nos.

11. Telemarketing is generally very effective for setting an appointment only if you learn that that's *all* you should do by phone in such a case. If you are setting appointments for an in-person sales call, then don't ever get into talking specifics, quoting prices, and so on. Only after a personal sales call can you bring your prospect to a buying stage for many products and services. When asked specific questions, acknowledge them and say they will be answered in person. When setting appointments, don't allow yourself to be trapped into giving your sales talk on the phone.

12. Keep your calls brief, business-like, and to the point. Nearly everyone will appreciate that. Remember that people lead busy lives and are only talking to you because you are promising some benefit. Don't lose the opportunity because you became distracted.

13. Never forget the saying "People don't buy for your reasons, they buy for theirs." If you call someone, talk in terms of benefits to that person.

14. Don't assume the prospect understands you correctly. Always repeat key times and places for an appointment.

15. Avoid any debates or arguments. You'll only force a prospect to defend his or her position.

16. Telemarketing is not the time to make idle conversation or to express your personal views on anything. To do so is unprofessional. You should be on the phone just a few minutes to obtain an appointment, no more than four or five to sell something.

17. Understand that there are some people you can't reach, no matter what you say or do. While they represent a very small percentage of the people you call, many beginners focus on

them and feel frustrated if they don't achieve perfect results. These are the salespeople who burn out very quickly. As with all forms of selling, telemarketing is a numbers game.

18. Accept the fact that most people you call are not going to be very good prospects. If you keep getting resistance then terminate the call politely and go on to the next. Getting involved in verbal fencing matches is bad for your self-esteem. A few of those encounters and you're ready to throw in the towel. Good telemarketing is using the law of averages to your best advantage.

A TELEMARKETING "SECRET" YOU MUST UNDERSTAND

Let me share a secret with you that all sales pros know quite well and beginners have a tough time understanding. The world is loaded, and I do mean loaded, with prospects. They are a dime a dozen. You can't really ruin anything with a bad sales call. It's impossible to waste good prospects because there's no such thing except in your mind. They are simply prospects, nothing more. Just learn from your error so you don't repeat it and continue on. If one prospect doesn't work out, there are always two more to take that person's place.

Always remember that no matter what you sell, somewhere in this country, in your state, in your city are lots of people who would love to hear from you and buy from you. There are plenty of them right in the area you live in. It's your job to find them.

10

Setting Sales Appointments by Telemarketing

The information I've shared with you so far applies to all telemarketing. In this chapter I will show you strategies to set effective sales appointments, and in Chapter 11 I will show you how to sell products and services by telephone.

I've separated this material because different strategies and approaches are required to perform each method successfully. The telemarketing call for a sales appointment is a very brief call. It's brief because if you want an appointment to see someone you can't tell this person too much or he or she will make a value judgment right on the phone. Since this person knows very little at that point, it's very difficult to get an appointment.

Telemarketing, because it is so popular today, is getting a little harder to do, especially when you are calling business firms. You often have to get past receptionists and secretaries, whom I refer to as gatekeepers. In some firms these people are trained to weed out sales calls before the decision maker is connected. At the end of this chapter I've outlined some very effective strategies to deal with this problem.

Another difficulty is getting past the voice-mail electronic answering systems. Again, at the end of this chapter, after the gatekeeper information, I've outlined a series of effective strategies for dealing with voice-mail systems.

To telemarket effectively for setting appointments, there are several big issues to settle. Let's cover them one at a time. They are:

1. Your work space
2. Your tools
3. Your prospect list
4. Your telemarketing script
5. Your time frame

YOUR WORK SPACE

A work space for effective telemarketing needs as much privacy as possible for two reasons. First, when you call someone, background noises, such as people speaking, other phones ringing, and so on, will distract your prospect from what you are saying. Since you only have a few seconds of his or her attention to start with, this can be a serious issue.

Some people telemarket from their home, which is perfectly okay. However, under no circumstances do you want the people you are calling to know that. A TV or radio playing, or kid noises in the background are signals to the prospects that you are an amateur. They lose respect for both you and the sales message you are delivering.

The second reason is for your own comfort. Constant distractions reduce the effectiveness of your efforts. Since telemarketing means hearing a lot of nos, it can get a little depressing. You must have your attention focused entirely on your telemarketing efforts so you can pull out of the little slumps that are bound to come along.

In addition, your work space needs to be physically comfortable. You'll be doing this two to four hours at a stretch and balancing a phone book, telephone, pad, and pencil in your lap for that long just doesn't cut it. Good seating, a table or desk space, and good lighting are a must.

YOUR TOOLS

Before you make your first call, you need to have everything in place. The art of successful telemarketing means being able to make call after call just as quickly as possible, with all your mental efforts focused. You can't be jumping up every few minutes to find supplies.

Following is a list of what I'd suggest for supplies. Add to it as necessary.

- At least two good ballpoint pens
- Two No.-2 pencils with erasers for making temporary notations
- Paper clips
- A roll of adhesive tape
- A stapler
- Several packs of blank 3 × 5 or 4 × 6 white index cards
- A 3 × 5 or 4 × 6 card-file box
- A pack of dividers for the file box showing the 12 months
- A second pack of dividers for the file box with the numbers 1–31
- Notepaper (I prefer legal pads)
- A 12-month calendar
- If you use an appointment book it needs to be included. Otherwise, get a book to record *all* your appointments. You don't want to schedule a telemarketing appointment and then find out you had some other event scheduled at the same time in a different book.

If you plan to use a computer for telemarketing then you need software designed for telemarketing purposes. Many people buy what is called "contact management" software and try to use it for telemarketing. Contact software is designed for keeping appointments and contacting people, but it doesn't have all the features needed for extensive telemarketing.

With a large database of prospects in it you'll be spending all sorts of time doing computer tasks to keep the thing going, time you should be spending making telemarketing calls. Purchase software designed specifically for telemarketing or use a manual system with the index cards.

One great tool for telemarketing is the telephone headset. You can buy this at most major office supply stores or through catalogs. It consists of a small box-shaped unit with the telephone keypad and a separate headset. It plugs into your regular telephone jack at home or single-line jack at work.

If you have a multiple-line telephone system, you can contact the manufacturer to purchase a headset for one of your existing phones. The ability to look things up and write with both hands free while speaking on the phone is a great benefit. I strongly suggest you consider a headset for telemarketing purposes.

Other useful tools are directories. Often you can't create prospect lists that are as complete as you need, either missing a telephone number or the name of the decision maker or not containing enough information to help you decide if you even want to call this prospect. At the very least you should have a set of local area telephone directories. If you have any other directories for the industry, they also belong by the telephone while telemarketing.

Also, keep the telephone numbers of local libraries available. You can call their reference department in the event you need a little additional information before making a call.

A word of caution: Don't prepare your prospect list research as you telemarket. Do it another time. It's okay to call a library once or twice while you're telemarketing to get some information, but if you have to do this frequently, then stop telemarketing and prepare a better calling list. Telemarketing requires a concentrated effort. You can't be jumping back and forth and still be effective.

YOUR PROSPECT LIST

To develop lists to call from, reread the earlier chapters on prospecting. Make a list large enough and include sufficient information so you can make the calls one right after the other, without stopping.

It's not good to attempt to qualify too heavily on the phone while setting appointments. Instead, prequalify when you prepare your prospect list. Take the time to locate reference material that will give you proper information to reach the decision makers you need.

While it does not work all the time, one of the best prospect resources you'll find is the telephone book. Everyone with a listed telephone number is included. Anytime I need a prospecting reference I consider this source first.

One of the big shortfalls of using a regular phone book is that it does not enable you to call only those prospects in a limited geographical area. However, if you know the telephone prefixes for the geographical area you want to limit yourself to, just call those. Many white-page telephone directories have a listing of the general areas certain prefixes cover. While it's often not exact, since the phone book is free and immediately available, it may be worth trying anyway.

A second shortfall is that when you're calling business firms out of a phone book, you don't know who to ask for. Sometimes knowing the decision maker's actual name in advance is really critical to success and you must use more detailed reference materials. But before you give up, if you can sell to a large prospect base and don't mind a few rude receptionists, there's a way around this problem. Sometimes it is just as effective to use a free source and put up with a little inconvenience than it is to spend money and time developing a more detailed prospect list. (And never forget, time is money.)

Finding the Buyer on a Cold Phone Call from the Phone Book

If you are selling an office-cleaning service, you might ask the receptionist, "Who is the person in your company who hires office-cleaning services?" Since you've just spilled the beans, chances increase she may brush you off with, "We are all set, thank you." But again, this is all a numbers game, nothing more. Many people won't respond like that. She may have heard the boss complaining about the filthy windows yesterday and connect you to his office. She may simply tell you the name of the person she thinks is the right one such as the Office Manager, Building Maintenance Manager, or perhaps the company President, and connect you.

Another strategy, if you know the job title of the decision maker you'll need, is to ask by job title. "May I speak to the Office Manager, please?"

Consider what it takes to develop a prospect list for telemarketing purposes other than the local phone book and weigh the options before you spend any money on lists.

YOUR TELEMARKETING SCRIPT

The Formula—Setting Appointments

Setting appointments by telephone is a totally different kind of sales call from actually selling something.

When you make a sales appointment, you simply introduce yourself to the decision maker and tell this person that you want to see him or her about the most important benefit your product or service offers. *Nothing else.* Be prepared that curiosity alone will compel most people to ask all sorts of questions. To make this work, you must never answer anything. Just tell them you need to see them about the benefit and close again for an appointment.

The fatal flaw most newcomers make is trying to answer questions. The minute you weaken and do this, the phone call is lost.

Keep in mind, if the strongest benefit you can offer does not compel someone to see you for five minutes, you are wasting your time. The chances of selling this person, no matter what you say or do, are slim. The key qualifier is that when you get a person on the phone who reacts positively to your best benefit, you have a person who most likely has a serious concern or interest in that benefit. The appointments you do get will have a serious interest in what your product or service offers. Therefore, assuming you know how to make a good sales presentation, your closing rate will skyrocket. Here's the formula for setting appointments:

1. The opening
2. Qualifying I have the actual decision maker
3. Stating the benefit
4. Asking for the appointment
5. Handle objections, restate the benefit, and close again (and again and again, etc.)

A word of warning. Always use a script for both your sales talk and for handling objections. Otherwise you'll be making unconscious changes as you call. Additionally, when prospects on the phone are objecting, it's very hard to remember all the answers.

A good telemarketing script to set an appointment is fast and brief. A rule you can never break is this: Never try to sell your product or service on the phone. Just sell the appointment, nothing else. Like most repeatable acts, it's a simple formula that works time after time.

The only time you'll have trouble with this formula is when you start to enhance it or allow the prospect to draw you into a conversation that becomes a sales talk. Also, don't change the order of these steps. Keep in mind, "If it's not broken, don't fix it!"

Here's a real-life example of how this formula might sound if you were selling sales-training service as I do.

> *Me*: "I'm calling about a program that will have your salespeople closing 50 percent more sales than they do today."
>
> *Me*: "Mr. _____ , my name is Ted Tate of Tate & Associates. We specialize in showing salespeople how to increase their closing ratios by at least 50 percent, often more."
>
> *Me*: "Mr. _____ , the reason I called you today is that I'd like to stop by for five minutes to show you, specifically, how I can increase the sales-closing ratios of your salespeople by at least 50 percent."
>
> *Me*: "I can see you at 10:00 A.M. on Thursday morning, or would sometime on Friday be better for you?" (wait for response)
>
> (*Note*: At this point, even a good prospect will probably raise an objection. It is just too fast for many people to absorb. That's why you must repeat the key benefit of what you do *three* times, otherwise it really doesn't register with a lot of people.)
>
> *Prospect*: "Well, tell me this. What does this program cost, just generally?"
>
> *Me*: "Mr. _____ , if I can't prove to you this will increase your salespeople's closing ratios by at least 50 percent you won't be spending a dime! I can see you either sometime Wednesday or Thursday at 10:00 A.M. Which do you prefer?"
>
> *Prospect*: "Send me some literature and I'll take a look at it."
>
> *Me*: "I can understand why you would ask me to do that. To be honest, this program isn't something we sell by mail order. We need to meet in person to discuss your business and sales goals

in order to increase your salespeople's closing ratios by at least 50 percent. Does Thursday at 10:00 A.M. look good, or would sometime Friday afternoon be better?"

Prospect: "I'm really booked up for the next few weeks. Call me the middle of next month for an appointment."

Me: "I can understand you're busy. With this new program, so am I. Instead of wasting time calling back and forth, get out your calendar. Let's set a specific appointment to discuss how I can increase your sales-closing ratios by at least 50 percent. If something changes, we can rearrange then. What day next month would be best? The tenth or the fifteenth?"

Prospect: "Tell me a little of what this is about."

Me: "I'd love to, but there's something you must see. Look, I'm sure you value your time just as much as I value mine. If I wasn't confident I could increase your sales-closing ratios by at least 50 percent I wouldn't be asking for the appointment."

"I'll make you a promise. If I'm in your office more than five minutes, it will be because you want me to be. Which of the days I mentioned looks good on your calendar, Thursday or Friday?"

Prospect: "Thursday."

Me: "What time are you looking at?"

Prospect: "10:00 A.M. is okay."

Me: "Great, I'll see you at 10:00 A.M. on Thursday the twenty-first. By the way, I almost forgot to ask. Are you the only person responsible for purchasing sales training services at _____ Company or is someone else involved in the decision process?"

Prospect: "That's me. I'm President so I'm the only one."

Me: "Fantastic. It will be nice to work with someone who can make a business decision without consulting a committee. I'll look forward to our meeting Thursday at 10:00 A.M. Have a great day."

On paper this looks like a lot, but it's really very brief. Read through it with a friend playing the part of the prospect and time it.

Because it is fast I repeated key information as I spoke. Many people don't think this fast. If you repeat, in a conversational way, the key benefit a few times, they will warm up to you and the idea of an appointment as the key benefit starts to register.

Your Personal Appointment Script Formula

Get out a pad and paper. Use the following formula to write your own personal appointment-setting script:

The Opening I'll Use

"Good (morning/afternoon), Mr./Ms. _____ . My name is (last name, then first and last name) of _____ ."

_____

_____

The Qualifier I'll Use

"Are you the person responsible for purchasing _____ ?"
  Must be unequivocal, otherwise:
  "Who, besides yourself, is responsible for making the final decision about buying _____ ?" *After response:* "Anyone else?"

_____

_____

The Benefit I'll Use

"Mr./Ms. _____ , the reason I'm calling is that we have a way for you to _____ ." *Your best benefit.* I want to stop by to see you for a few minutes and show you how _____ ." *Repeat same best benefit.*

_____

_____

The Close I'll Use

"I can see you (*specific*) Tuesday at 2:00 P.M. or sometime (*nonspecific*) Wednesday, which would be best for you?

_____

_____

If You Don't Get Objections with This, Check to See
if They Are Still Breathing

In the first script where I used myself as an example, I've illustrated for you the most common objections (except "I'm not interested," which is explained next): "How much is it?" "Tell me more details," "Send me some literature," "Call me next month for an appointment," and also an answer for what I knew this person was thinking but didn't mention, that I was blowing smoke and would waste a lot of his or her time. Rarely do people state all these objections on any one call; most people will only give you one or two.

The one objection I didn't cover is "I'm not interested." The reason I didn't is that, if you follow my advice about the other objections, then 95 out of 100 prospects won't have the nerve to say it. How can someone tell you, and mean it honestly, that he or she is not interested in closing 50 percent more sales (or whatever your biggest benefit is)? So long as you don't get into anything but the major benefit you offer, you won't hear "I'm not interested" very often.

If someone does say this, chances are you are speaking to someone who has no authority to buy and couldn't care less about the company or its success. Either that or this person simply doesn't believe you. If someone says that to me, my response would be:

Prospect: "I'm not interested."

Me: "Tell me, Mr. _____ , are you the person responsible for purchasing training services at your company?"

Me: (If yes) "Mr. _____ , you either think I'm lying or you don't really care how well your salespeople succeed. Which is it?"

Prospect: "Well, 50 percent is just hard to believe. We get calls like this all day and if I saw every salesperson who called, that's all I'd ever do."

Me: "I appreciate your honesty. I'm glad to hear you do care about the success of your salespeople. Please know that if I make an appointment with you, based on this claim of increasing your salespeople's closing ratio by 50 percent or better, and can't prove it, I'm the big loser. I'll be spinning my wheels for absolutely nothing.

Me: "Look, If I'm in your office more than five minutes it will be because you want me there. You really have nothing to lose and an awful lot to gain. Would Thursday be okay, or do you prefer Friday?

Remember, never give in. Just keep reminding the prospect of the key benefit, which, by itself, is very compelling. The reason people resist is this: *These people don't believe you and they are looking for an excuse to get rid of you.* As long as you don't give in to temptation to send literature, quote ballpark prices, and so on, you have a chance.

The more you keep repeating the key benefit the more it starts to grow on them. They begin to wonder if perhaps you could help them. They see your persistence as your own personal belief that you really can help them.

The minute you even give partial answers to any questions you'll lose this opportunity. Notice also that after each answer I finished by offering a choice. That makes it very hard for people not to answer. It also is hard for people to ignore and ask another question. Here's a list of common objections you'll get with this script.

Objection Responses

Expect objections! When you call people with such a vague request, it's only normal. The secret is to answer, then remind them they are interested in (your benefit), and close for another appointment. Don't quit until you have received five nos.

What Are You Selling? (What Is It?)

"I'm sure there are several questions you'd want answered about how _____ (*your big benefit*) can apply to your business specifically. That's why it's best we spend five minutes together. Would _____ o'clock on _____ day be okay, or do your prefer sometime _____ day?"

Send Me Some Literature

"Mr./Ms. _____ , I wish it were that simple, but there's something I have to show you about _____ (*your big benefit*). Would sometime on _____ day be okay, or would you prefer _____ o'clock on _____ day?"

I'm Too Busy to See You, Just Send Me Something

"Mr./Ms. _____ , what I hear you saying is that you are busy and you are not convinced that if we meet I can really _____ (*your big benefit*). Is that a fair statement?" (*wait for answer*)

"Mr./Ms. _____ , I'm a salesperson and my time is just as valuable to me. I know that if I make an appointment to see you based on the premise that _____ (*your big benefit*), and I can't, I'm making a trip for nothing. I know right now that I can deliver on that promise."

"All I'm asking for is five minutes. If I'm there any longer, it's only because you will have asked me to stay. Would _____ o'clock on _____ day be good, or should I make it _____ day?"

I'm Really Busy Right Now, Call Me in Two Weeks

"I understand how that can be. Let me make a suggestion so we don't wind up in a game of telephone tag. Let's set a specific day and time for two weeks from now and then if anything comes up, we can change it. I'm looking at my calendar for the week of the _____ . Would _____ o'clock on _____ day be okay, or do your prefer sometime _____ day?"

How Much Is It?

"Mr./Ms. _____ , I honestly wish I could answer that but I'd need the answers to a few questions first. I do know that it's proven to be very cost effective. Would _____ o'clock on _____ day be good, or should I make it _____ day?"

Just Stop by When You Are in the Neighborhood

"Great, but just to save your time as well as mine, let's pick a specific day and time right now. Would _____ 'clock on _____ day be okay, or do you prefer sometime _____ day?"

BE ASSERTIVE TO SUCCEED

Is this high-pressure selling? No, I don't believe so. It is assertive selling. I suggest this simply because over many years of dealing with people I've found that unless salespeople can be assertive they are doomed to failure. People who are afraid to be assertive tell themselves that others will get mad or upset, that it's not nice to speak to others that way.

Fortunately that's just not true. Certainly, a few people may feel annoyed, but what really happens is that as you continue being persistent, people start to question their own judgment. They start to wonder if they shouldn't investigate what you are suggesting. Your very act of being assertive comes across as a strong belief in what you sell.

When you first approach people, in person or by telephone, their defenses go up. They offer initial resistance almost automatically. At that point, they are not sure themselves; they don't have enough information to evaluate your offer. That's where requests for more information or literature or costs come from.

You may not believe me if you are new to selling, but you have these people at their weakest moment. They are resisting seeing you but deep down inside, because you've just stated a key benefit that really is valid and important to them, they fear making a mistake. So long as you stand your ground and only restate your key benefit and nothing else and decline to accept the resistance they throw at you, they have a big conflict going on inside. You may really have something of value they want. The more you stand your ground for a specific appointment, the more they doubt their own position—the more they wonder if they shouldn't see you.

On the other hand, if they resist and you back off, they tend to believe their first judgment was correct, that you are offering nothing of value to them.

If you believe that you are the only person in this world who has doubts, unanswered questions, and even fears about what you are doing everyday, you're not in touch with reality. *Everybody* has these concerns, from world leaders who run nations to homeless people in your city. Some people just hide it a little better than others. This is why assertive selling works.

Again, I will remind you that there is a fine line between being aggressive and assertive. Never cross that line. The minute you become aggressive or verbally abusive, people get defensive and immediately retreat. So long as you remain positive and nonthreatening, but assertive, you will succeed.

GETTING PAST THE GATEKEEPER

There is an art to getting past secretaries, receptionists, assistants, and others who make a big deal out of your speaking to the decision maker. Don't blame these people for ruining your life. Keep in mind that the huge number of telemarketing calls made to companies becomes a burden.

If the decision makers of the world took every telephone call that came in for them, they would do nothing all day but speak on the telephone. As a top executive in several different firms over the years, take my word for it: Telemarketing calls can become a big distraction. There will be some people you can't reach, no matter how clever you get. You have two choices. You can get all bent out of shape, ranting and raving (or just depressed) about how unfair life is. This of course prevents you from being as effective on your next call.

Your second choice is to recall the sales slogan, "Who cares?" This is another way to say "Life is, always has been, and will continue to be 'unfair'. It is beyond my power to change anything *except* my own behavior and feelings. I accept the fact that I can't win every time. In truth, it doesn't matter (who cares?). Getting upset or feeling bad is a drain on my energy and ability to make other sales calls. All the energy I use for that negative behavior is wasted. It does nothing to help me attain my sales goals. I know that the law of averages is in my favor if I continue my sales efforts."

With that in mind, here are some effective tactics for reaching people on the phone who are hard to get.

Often, in many companies, telephone systems have a specific extension number, which can be accessed by an outside caller (*if* you know the extension number).

Let's say you are calling Bill Jones, VP of Marketing for XYZ Company. When you call the main switchboard number and ask for Bill Jones, the operator puts you through to his secretary's desk, not his. Frequently the switchboard won't give you the direct-dial number for the buyer's desk because they have been warned not to. The secretary will then proceed to qualify who you are and what you want.

Six Tactics to Obtain a Direct Extension Number

Strategy 1

This works because while secretaries and receptionists are highly trained to block sales calls to the boss, the rest of the company couldn't care less. With this strategy you call the wrong department, say Shipping. Don't lie, but act like you are an employee who just got the wrong extension. Needless to say this only works when calling larger firms. You must act very matter-of-fact and never get upset. The call goes like this:

"Shipping, Mary speaking."

"Oops, I think I got the wrong extension. I take it you are not Bill Jones" (say it like a little joke).

"Not hardly. This is Shipping."

"Sorry to bother you. My records are all messed up. I show this as Bill Jones' extension. Say, you don't happen to have it there, do you?"

(*if no*): "Darn it. Anyone else there know it, just to save me a few steps?"

What you are hoping for is that someone has a company list or directory of inside extension numbers. Many people will look up the number for you if they feel they are helping out a fellow employee. Just be low key. In a really big company you can call different departments until it works.

Strategy 2

Call the top executive's office. Chances are you'll get his or her secretary. Don't imply you are an employee in this case. The secretary to the company president may figure you out. You can, however, imply that you know the person you want to reach rather well by using this person's first name. The secretary will be more apt to get you through. The call might go like this:

Secretary: "Frank Jackson's office, Eva Peterson speaking."

You: "Oops, I think I made a mistake. I show this number for Bill Jones' personal extension. I guess this isn't Bill's personal extension and you aren't Bill."

Secretary: "No, this is the President's office. I'm his secretary."

You: "Gee, I'm sorry to bother you. I didn't mean to do that."

Secretary: "No problem. Would you like me to switch you to the receptionist?"

You: "Thanks. Maybe you could do me a small favor to save some time. What's Bill's correct personal extension number?"

A few points. First, I'm being humble so the secretary feels a sense of importance. Second, I'm being humorous so she feels this is not of any great importance. It makes her more apt to grant me the small favor. Third, the "save some time" adds a little urgency, so she may act without really thinking about what's going on. Fourth, I used the term "personal extension number" twice. That's so she doesn't give me the guy's secretary. Fifth, she may not be willing to give the extension number out. If she says that I say: "I understand, look, can you just connect me then? I'm running a little late."

Strategy 3

Another tactic to get past "gatekeepers" is to call very early or very late. Nearly all gatekeepers will arrive a little before company opening time and leave around closing time.

Some executives like to arrive early, before the day's business gets going, to have time to handle some business in peace. Other executives tend to stay late.

Try placing your call to the prospect before opening or after closing. Sometimes the decision maker is the *only* one there to answer the phone.

Strategy 4

Often, in calling companies, you don't have the name of the person you need to speak to. If you ask the receptionist for a name and then ask her to put you through, she may tip off the person or the person's secretary that a salesperson is on the phone.

It's always best to get the name of the person you need, thank the person who gave it to you, then hang up. Call back in an hour and ask for the person by name. At a busy switchboard, they'll never remember your voice.

Strategy 5

To get the name of the person you need to speak with, play dumb. Act a little confused.

You: "Excuse me, is a Joe Fabeits your Vice President of Sales?"

Receptionist: "Joe who? We have no one working here by that name. What did you need?"

You: "I'm sending him some information he requested, but I can't read the name. How does your VP of Sales spell his name?"

Receptionist: "B-r-o-w-n. Brown. It's a woman; her first name is Anne."

You: "Great, thanks for your assistance."

Strategy 6

Sometimes when you start out just asking for the name of the President (or title of the person you need to speak with) the receptionist may want to know why you are asking or may connect you to the Personnel Department or the person's secretary, who also will give you the third degree.

Ask the receptionist for a correct mailing address instead:

You: "Hi, I need to verify your correct mailing address please."

Receptionist: "That would be 1234 Main Street."

You: "And the zip code?"

Receptionist: "12345."

You: "Great! Thanks for your help. Oh, by the way, what's the right spelling of the President's last name?"

Receptionist: "Smith. S-M-I-T-H."

You: "First name?"

Receptionist: "Joe. J-O-E."

If the receptionist says "Don't you know the President's name?" make up a name, tell it to her, and end with a question. "We show a Joe Fabeits, right?" She'll correct you with the right one. The reason this works is you start out with a very innocent request for an address. By the time you ask what you really want to know, the name of the President, she has calls coming in that she has to answer. It's easier to tell you than to argue. In addition, once a person starts answering a string of questions, it's hard to stop.

Don't ask to speak to that person now. The receptionist may tip him or her off that it's a salesperson on the phone. Just thank the receptionist, hang up, and call your prospect back after a little time has passed. The receptionist gets all kinds of calls and so long as you act like it's no big deal and are polite, she'll never remember you.

Some Examples of Getting Past the Gatekeeper

1. Ask for a person by name, as if you know him or her. Instead of, "May I speak to William Smith, please?" say:

   "Bill Smith, please" or just "Bill Smith."

   (If you overdo being polite you sound like an outsider.)

2. Answer each question the secretary asks you, but then end with your own question. This keeps pressure where it belongs, on her.

3. Most secretaries will quit after two or three exchanges and let the boss deal with it.

   You: "Bill Smith, please."

   Secretary: "May I say who is calling?"

   You: "This is Ted Tate, is Bill Smith in?"

   Secretary: "I'll see, may I tell him what this is regarding?"

   You: "This is a business matter. Is Bill in or should I call back?"

   Try to avoid giving your company name. Here's an example:

   You: "Bill Smith, please."

   Secretary: "May I tell Mr. Smith who is calling?"

   You: "Ted Tate. Is he in?"

   Secretary: "I'll see. What company are you with, Mr. Tate?"

You: "This is a business matter between myself and Bill Smith. Is he in or can you tell me when I might reach him?"

Secretary: "May I tell Mr. Smith what this is in regard to?"

You: "I understand. Please connect me to Bill Smith."

Secretary: "Mr. Smith likes to know who is calling and what for. What is this regarding?"

You: "It's important I talk to Bill Smith now. It's okay if you put me through. I'll assume full responsibility. Please connect me now."

4. Once you get past the secretary, treat it like any other call. Never mention any problem in getting through.

5. Another method is to refer to a nonexistent letter:

   You: "I'm calling regarding a letter. Is he in?"

   If the secretary comes back and says: "Mr. Smith doesn't have any correspondence from you. What is this regarding?"

   You: "Sure he does. Put him on the phone. He'll remember."

   If Bill Smith comes to the phone and asks you what letter, just say you recently sent him a letter regarding (benefit). Then make a remark such as "Well, you know how the post office is. Anyway, here's why I called..."

6. When questioned by a secretary some telemarketers will simply say:

   You: "It's a personal matter. Is he in or should I call back?"

   The reason this works is that most gatekeepers do not want to offend the top executive in their company by prying into a personal matter.

GETTING PAST DREADED VOICE MAIL

Voice mail, as with all modern electronic marvels, has a lot of positive features. Unfortunately, its downside is that it limits human communication considerably. For individuals with an emergency or rush situation it can be very frustrating to get lost in a voice-mail system. For those in some form of sales, it can be maddening to call people continuously only to reach one voice-mail system after another.

In my business as a sales and marketing consultant I've dealt with quite a few different methods of dealing with these systems. The problem is a complex one. Keep in mind that no one method works every time. Why? One reason is that there are several different kinds of voice-mail systems in use, each working a little differently than others. Another reason is the human factor. People have numerous valid and not-so-valid reasons for not answering voice mail.

For instance, many people abuse the use of voice mail by never answering their phone. It becomes another way to not work at work. In other cases I've seen employers install voice mail then cut back the number of employees. Each employee becomes so overloaded with work he or she can't possibly answer the phone each time it rings. There are many other reasons, so callers must be resourceful and persistent in order to get past voice mail.

Seven Successful Techniques of Getting Past Voice Mail

Success Method 1

If you keep getting a person's voice mail without response, try to reach a live attendant. In many (not all) voice-mail systems if you press the zero key on a Touch-Tone phone, you'll get connected to a live operator on duty (if it's during normal business hours and there is such a person). Also, nearly all systems are designed to work for people who still own a rotary phone and can't use voice mail. If you simply don't press any buttons when asked, eventually you'll be connected to a live operator.

My technique with the operator is this (spoken quickly, before she reconnects me into the voice-mail system again): I say "I need a little help before you connect me. I'm calling for Mary Jones and I keep getting her voice mail. Can you please tell me if she's in today? Also, if she is, is there any way you can page her?"

If your party isn't really in, then you might ask the operator to tell you who is in that you can speak with now. A secretary, co-worker, or supervisor can at least tell you the best way to reach this person. In some cases, these people may be a better choice. Remember, one live human voice is worth two voices in the voice-mail system!

Success Method 2

Be persistent. Actually, just be a cheerful nag. If you repeat your message every day on voice mail, he or she will get the message. After the third time I'll say something along these lines: "Mary, this is my third message, I'd really appreciate your call back. Thanks." Never, never allow any anger in your voice, just a slight questioning tone as if you are puzzled as to why this person hasn't returned your call. Always go out of your way to sound upbeat and cheerful (especially if this is call five or six). Then add a little gentle nudge such as "Gee, I hope your voice mail's working, this is my fifth call!" or "Boy, you must be really busy, this is my fourth call." You might say, "I'd really appreciate a call back today, this is my third call. Thanks."

Success Method 3

Use urgency and/or time limits. This is a very successful technique used frequently by collection agencies. By law they can't leave threatening messages on answering machines and voice mail, so in order to get the deadbeats to call back, they'll say something such as, "I need to speak with you before noon, please call me by then." Or, "This is an important business matter, please call me by five o'clock today. Thanks."

If you use this method, be sure to have a valid reason when he or she calls back; otherwise the person will get angry and you lose the opportunity you just created. For instance, if you sell something your excuse might be a sale or special that ends soon.

Success Method 4

Say nothing but your name and phone number. "Please call me, John Smith, at 555–1234" (or just use your first name and phone number). Many people will call just to see who you are. By not identifying your reason for the call, they can't be sure of its importance.

This method does not work too well if you do it just once or twice because if people don't recognize your name, they tend not to call you back. *However*, this works very well if you *keep* doing it since the recipients start to worry that they may be missing an important message.

Success Method 5

Spill the beans. Sometimes the best method is the direct one. Instead of spending time trying to get past voice mail, use it to your advantage. Write a quick, dynamic sales talk and leave it on voice-mail systems. Here's how:

1. Be brief. Some systems cut off automatically, so write out and rehearse your sales talk with a watch. I'd keep it under a minute.

2. Make it dynamic by stressing your biggest, best benefit, two at the most. Forget who you are (except for name, company name, and phone number) and stress how they will benefit by calling you back.

3. Add urgency by telling them why they need to call now (a sale, discount, special offer, or something that ends soon).

4. Promise brevity. Do you know the main reason people dread talking on the phone to salespeople? They can't get off. This is a big reason people use voice mail, just to avoid long-winded calls. When writing telemarketing scripts for my clients, I often suggest a line such as " ... if you call me back, we'll both know if this applies to you in the first two or three minutes. I'm sure the opportunity to (*benefit they'll achieve*) is worth just a few minutes."

5. Repeat your name and phone number twice. Once at the beginning, once at the end, just in case the voice mail shuts off before you finish your message.

Success Method 6

When you get a voice-mail recording, state your name and phone number first, before anything else. Then continue to speak but

My Daily Telemarketing Success Guide

Today's date _____

My goal, this session, is _____ completed calls (or more)

# Voice mail messages; answering machines; lines busy; line disconnects	
# Dials	
# Completed calls	
# Appointments	

Instructions:

As you make your telephone calls, place a hash mark showing results in the appropriate box.

Don't quit until you've reached your goal of completed calls.

DIALS = where someone answers, but you don't speak to the decision maker

COMPLETED CALLS = when you speak to the decision maker

APPOINTMENTS = setting a specific day and time to see the decision maker

My daily telemarketing success guide.

disconnect the call in mid-sentence. The person receiving the call will think he or she has missed something due to a faulty voice mail and will call back to see what it's about. Here's the script:

"Hello, this is Sam Jones. My phone number is 555–1234. Can you … "<cut-off>.

Success Method 7

Just leave a straight message and see if you get a call back. All these other techniques are time consuming. In business and in selling, time is money. Despite its drawbacks, most people will call you back if you leave a message on their voice mail, so why burn time playing games? Save your energy and time for the ones who don't and who are worth investing the effort.

A basic rule when calling: Don't insult people or make disparaging remarks about their "stupid voice-mail system." They think it's a good idea or they wouldn't have it. I always act like I don't even notice any problem (which *is* acting if you've just spent 30 minutes getting jerked around in their voice-mail system).

Starting a conversation on a negative note is a good way to get turned down for whatever you are calling for. Keep your emotions bottled up. The instant you get angry out of frustration, you lose.

11

Selling Products and Services by Telephone

This is a different ball game from setting sales appointments, with new rules. I'm big on reducing things down to formulas. I find people can understand how to apply new techniques and ideas to their personal needs if they are broken down into formulas. I've done so with this telemarketing chapter on selling products and services by telephone.

There are two formulas. The first one is so you can write, as you read, your first telemarketing script. The second formula is to give you ways to handle objections and other resistance. You write these on a separate page and keep them by your phone as you call. When someone raises an objection, gives you a stalling tactic or resistance, you'll be confident, knowing exactly how to handle it, exactly what to say, just as the professionals do.

Each part of the formula is explained, examples are given, and you are invited to write out examples that would apply to your own personal selling situation. By the time you are finished with this chapter, you can write out your own personal telemarketing script, ready to go. However, I'd like to ask a small favor of you: *Please, don't write in this book*.

Even if you own this book, don't write in it. Make copies and fill in the blanks on those. Telemarketing scripts are not cast in stone. They take testing, by making calls and then adjusting. If you write in the book, you'll have a hard time making changes because whatever gets written starts to be cast in stone and becomes very hard to discard, even if it's not working.

You need a free and open mind when you write these scripts. You need to be willing to experiment. A sales training student recently asked me, "What's the very best telemarketing script?" My answer, "The one that works best."

SALES SCRIPT FORMULAS FOR SELLING BY TELEPHONE

Here's the formula for writing a telemarketing script to sell products or services by telephone.

The Opening Statement

The first words you say and how you say them will make or break many telemarketing calls. Keep in mind that you called them, they didn't call you. If they want any cute remarks about the weather, breaking news, your kids, their kids, the secretary, the voice-mail system, or anything else, they have many friends and/or business associates who can handle that.

If you insist on sounding like a telemarketer, just start out by asking people "How are you today?" Coming from a total stranger over the telephone, it's an insincere and patronizing remark that turns most people off. Don't start off like that.

Many newcomers feel you have to build rapport with people first. Nonsense. Most people lead busy, sometimes confusing lives. You'll be more appreciated if you get to the point, do your business, and get off the phone, without any small-talk babble. A second sin is being too long-winded. Salespeople who don't have the nerve to use closes go on and on about features and benefits. They end up repeating the same phrases over and over.

A good script offers benefits and asks a series of trial closes. Rarely should you give every feature and benefit. A good opening will further cut down the need for long sales talks. Where the lines are indicated, fill in some examples of each kind of opening you might use.

Ask a Question That Illustrates a Benefit You Offer

"Ms. _____ , is your present mortgage rate over 7 percent?"

"Mr. _____ , are all your deliveries on time, with no customer complaints?"

"Mrs. _____ , if there were a way for you to (*benefit*), you'd like to know more about it, wouldn't you?"

Your Questions

1. _____

2. _____

3. _____

Give a Warning That Illustrates a Need for Your Service or Product

"Mr. _____ , I'm calling because there have been three burglaries in your area, one of them while the family was home."

"Ms. _____ , the Federal Reserve Bank has just raised interest rates. I wanted you to know what that will do to bond prices."

"Mrs. _____ , did you know that carpets that haven't been cleaned in over two years are breeding grounds for illness?"

Your Warnings

1. _____

2. _____

3. _____

Offer a Special Deal

"Mrs. _____ , I called to tell you how your family can save over 25 percent on weekly grocery bills."

"Mr. _____ , I'm calling to let you know how you can get (*benefit*) and save over 50 percent."

Your Specials

1. _____

2. _____

3. _____

Refer to Something or Someone They Know

"Ms. _____ , we were just working over at your neighbor's home and they (*benefit they received by doing business with you*)."

"Mrs. _____ , we're going to have a display at the _____ show this year along with some fabulous specials. Just so you don't miss out..."

Your "Refer" Openings

1. _____

2. _____

3. _____

Getting Attention Quickly

When you want an appointment to see a prospect, or to sell something, you need to think in his or her terms. Remember, people have all kinds of events going on in their lives. You need to break through that preoccupation barrier so they listen to what you have to say. That's why small talk can wipe you out. Get to the point quickly with one of these strategies. Fill in examples of each you can use.

1. Mention a Specific Problem You Solve

This is a powerful strategy because if prospects have such a problem, they'll want to see you. If they don't, they won't, which is okay also, since if people don't have a need for your service or product in the first place, chances of a sale are pretty slim.

"We're working with one of your neighbors because they were having problems (*fill in problem here; forget benefits, you are a problem solver*) and they decided we were the best equipped to (*restate problem here*). I thought I'd call to see if we could stop by and see if you have any concerns about (*restate problem again and mention a second if practical*)."

Your Example

_____

_____

_____

2. Mention a Unique Benefit/Feature

"We are the only waterproofing company with an unconditional lifetime guarantee."

Your Example

_____

_____

_____

3. Refer to Something Topical

"Have you read about the interest rates going up?"

Your Example

_____

_____

_____

4. Refer to Mailing

"I'm calling about the letter we mailed you recently."

Your Example

_____

_____

_____

5. Mention a Reference

"Jack Mason at ABC Manufacturing was so impressed he felt you'd want to know..."

Your Example

_____

_____

_____

6. Refer to a Personal Event or Situation

"Congratulations on your new baby (*graduation, promotion, wedding, etc.*)."

Your Example

_____

_____

_____

Making the Offer They Can't Refuse

When you call people on the telephone, you must reach them quickly or lose them. They always have the option of hanging up. Therefore, whatever you sell, or if you are trying to obtain an appointment to sell, the offer must be enticing (or at least sound enticing). Below are a few ideas to get you started. Don't be limited just to these. Sometimes it will take a little experimenting to find the right offer. Remember also that most major firms, such as retailers and manufacturers who make special offers, will have previously marked up the price to cover the special. Newcomers to business and many small businesspeople don't fully understand pricing strategies. They frequently price themselves out of business. No matter what you offer as a special, you are still entitled to make a fair profit.

The Free Gift

A free gift can be given when a purchase is made. You can also offer a free gift in exchange for an appointment, but be careful about too large a gift. People may start wondering just how much profit you make and can become wary. The best gifts will be directly connected to your product or service.

Your Example

_____

_____

_____

The Time Limit

You are making them a special offer that shortly expires. This gives people a reason to take immediate action.

Your Example

_____

_____

_____

The Special Price

Here you offer a discount. An explanation is sometimes offered, such as: only people reached by phone; people within a certain group; previous customers; or buy one, get one free. Often these special prices are used along with the time limit.

Your Example

_____

_____

_____

The Free Survey (or Estimate)

Often used to get an appointment. Usually offered without obligation.

Your Example

_____

_____

_____

The Home (Office) Trial

Here the prospect is allowed to try the product or service with the option of not paying if not satisfied after a trial period. It works, but there have been cases where it worked so well that companies went out of business. Not all businesses lend themselves to this kind of offer. A variation would be that the customer pays up front but can get a full refund within so many days if not satisfied. This might help (but not completely) keep out the insincere people who only want something for nothing. You could also charge for unreturnable materials, such as a free trial of a copy machine but customer agrees to pay for paper and toner supplies used.

Your Example

_____

_____

_____

The In-home (Office) Demonstration

If you sell something that lends itself to demonstration, this often has appeal—especially if the prospect is thinking about purchasing one anyway.

Your Example

_____

_____

_____

Dealing with Brush-Offs

This is where it gets interesting. A lot of inexperienced telemarketers fall by the wayside when prospects say "I'm not interested." The truth is, many times people say this almost involuntarily. They don't really know what else to say and perhaps you just interrupted some activity they'd like to get back to.

The trick is to back them down, but in a nice way so they feel comfortable. If your voice gets harsh or you use harsh words then they feel obligated to stand their ground. Here are a few examples:

"I can appreciate what you are saying, however..."

"You are interested in *(benefit)*..."

"If I could really show you a way to (benefit), you'd at least want to know more about it, right?"

"It's difficult for me to understand why you would say that, Ms. _____ , especially considering the fact that (*a client*) has had such a successful experience with us. Let me tell you about..."

"Mr. _____ of _____ Company said it was the best..."

"Considering the fact that we give you a 100 percent guarantee, no questions asked, doesn't it make sense to at least..."

"Look, I can understand you're a busy person. I'm sure you value your time as much as I value my own. However, if I can honestly *(benefit)*, it certainly makes sense to spend just a few minutes to find out how, doesn't it?"

Trouble Signs

Sometime prospects will give signals that they are resisting what we say. Here are some ways to identify possible resistance:

Silence

When you pause, they say nothing.

Vague Agreements

"If you say so." "Well, maybe." "I guess so."

Doubt

"That's hard to believe." "Really?"

Half-hearted Agreement

"Um hmmm." "Okay." "Yeah." "Maybe."

Negative Response to Your Offer

"It's way too big." "My cousin had one and hated it."

Qualify the Reason

When you recognize resistance, try to identify the real reason for it. Here are three techniques to do just that:

Question

Here you ask questions to define prospects' statements.
    "What do you think about..." or "How do you feel about..."

Restate

Repeat what the prospect has said, but as a question to gain further information.

Prospect: "I'm not really interested in insurance."
You: "You're not really interested in insurance?"

Your Example

_____

_____

_____

Restate

Here we slightly exaggerate the prospect's statement. The best approach is to select whatever benefit is gained from what he or she claims not to be interested in. You then ask if he or she is are also uninterested in that benefit.

Prospect: "I'm really not interested in insurance."

You: "You're not interested in providing financial security and protection for your family?"

Your Example

_____

_____

_____

Handling Resistance

Once you bring out resistance, you then need to resolve it. Here are a few techniques.

Answer directly: "We don't charge extra for delivery."

Ignore: If a prospect brings up a minor item, it may be best just to ignore the statement.

Turn an Advantage into a Disadvantage

Sometime people see things as disadvantages that may really have a positive side. In these cases, it's important to mention the good side.

"Sure, they weigh more than any other machine in that class. The shell is made of a superior material. Because of that, they won't be subject to breaking as do our competitors'."

Your Example

_____

_____

_____

Focus on a Positive Point

What if the resistance is negative with no real positive feature? Then use that to go into other, more positive features:

"The traffic at rush hour can be a little heavy at times, but this location is fantastic. Your children only have a short walk to school and safe playground facilities. Shopping is just a few minutes away."

Your Example

_____

_____

_____

Give Proof

Use statistics to prove your point:

"Last year over 1,000 of these units were placed in service. We are proud to say they have a 99 percent success rate."

Your Example

_____

_____

_____

Third-party Reference

"We cleaned the carpeting and living room furniture at Mrs. Jones' house on Beacon Street. She was so happy she wrote us a letter indicating her carpets and furniture hadn't been that clean since the day they were new."

Your Example

_____

_____

_____

Handling Objections

Two Secrets for Handling Objections

Newcomers to selling become discouraged with objections because they see them as rejection. Professionals understand that when people are going through a decision process, they will consider both positive and negative sides to the issue.

The first secret is to treat objections as a request for more information. The second secret is to have answers written out in advance of any sales calls, so you need not become flustered or distracted from continuing your sales talk after handling an objection.

The Success Formula

1. Listen carefully to what and how the objection is stated. Be sure you really understand.
2. Pause slightly before you answer.
3. Use a cushion of empathy.
4. Answer objection.
5. In the same breath, go for a trial close.

Cushion of Empathy Phrases

A cushion of empathy simply means you acknowledge the prospect's right to question and shows a sensitivity on your part. *Be very careful* how you say these phrases. You are not agreeing with the prospect. In fact, in the same breath you are going to tell the prospect why he or she is wrong. Never use the words, "I agree" or "I understand," because the prospect will think you are saying that he or she is right. It would be okay, however, to say, "I agree that a lot of people have said that; however, these recent statistics have proven..." or "I can understand why you might feel that way—I used to myself until I found out that..." or "I can appreciate your feelings; I thought something like that myself until I found out that..."

A cushion of empathy allows you to answer an objection gently without antagonizing the prospect. Because people may raise several objections, you need several cushions of empathy to avoid sounding like you rehearsed your sales talk.

"Mrs. _____ , I can appreciate what you are saying."

"Mr. _____ , I felt that way myself before I fully understood the program."

"Ms. _____ , that's an important issue."

"Mrs. _____ , I understand how someone might feel that way."

"Mr.———, I see the point you are making."

Your Own Cushions

"Mrs. _____ ,

_____

"Mr. _____ ,

_____

"Ms. _____ ,

_____

Dealing with Stalls and Put-Offs

An objection is when the person is flatly objecting to what you say. "It won't fit," "I don't have any money," "I don't like the color selection," and so on. A stall on the other hand is just that, usually some reason they can't buy now. They are not saying they don't want it, just deferring or stalling the decision. Stalls are the most common type of resistance. Here are some techniques to handle them. Add your own.

The Limited Offer

Whenever you can, something about your offer should have a limited time to help avoid the stall.

"Mr. _____ , this deal is only available through Friday. After that, prices increase 20 percent."

Your Offer

_____

_____

Offer a Credit Plan

"Ms. _____ , we accept Visa, MasterCard, and American Express."

or

"Mrs. _____ , we can give you 30-day billing."

Your Offer

_____

_____

Loss of Value

"By delaying membership in our swim club, you'll miss part of the season."

or

"The sooner we can schedule an estimate, the sooner we can let you know what problems may exist, if any."

Your Offer

_____

_____

Offer to Write a Smaller Deal

People usually hate to admit they can't afford something. Sometimes an offer to reduce the initial obligation will close a sale.

> "Let me suggest this Mr. _____ . I'll send you half a case at the single lot price to get you started. You'll still be saving and have an opportunity to try us immediately. You can order the larger quantities next time. Make sense?"

Your Offer

_____

_____

Offer to Write the Order Now and Process It Later

When someone tells you to call back in so many days, implying he or she will order then, respond with:

> "In order to save time, let me write that order now. I will schedule delivery next month. That way you'll get the special saving plan you'd miss next month."

Your Offer

_____

_____

Get a Commitment for a Callback

If you can't break through the stall, then ask for a commitment as to when you can call back for a decision. If they say they'll call, just tell them you're almost impossible to reach and you'll call them back in _____ days.

Learn to Hear Buying Signals

Probing

Ask your prospect questions as you mention benefits. Also ask questions after you answer an objection or stall. This allows you to gauge his or her degree of interest. Positive answers indicate a readiness to take action. Negative answers indicate additional resistance. End your statements with open-ended questions like these, then stop. Don't allow yourself to speak until the prospect has answered your question.

"... how does that sound?"

"... does that make sense?"

"... have I answered your question?"

"... any questions?"

Listen for Buying Signals

When prospects show a lot of interest and have questions, especially concerning possible ownership, *stop the sales pitch, no matter where you are in it!* It's time to go for a trial close. If they don't bite, just go on from there. These are examples of a prospect showing buying signals:

"How long does it take for delivery?"

"How does that have to be paid?"

"What's the warranty?"

"How do I know it would fit?"

Closing the Deal—Now!

Direct Question Close

When you are not sure where the prospect is in the selling process, but have no refusal to buy, sometimes the most effective technique is simply to ask for the order. If the prospect balks, then you will know where you are in the sale and deal with it. Here are a few examples:

"Can I write this up then?"
"Should I send it out?"

Your Direct Question Close(s)

_____

_____

Alternative (Choice) Close

Often prospects will show buying signals but may be a little uncomfortable in saying yes. An alternative close gives them choices, but whatever one they make, they have made a buying decision.

"Do you want this on a credit card or do you prefer to pay?"

"Which color do you want, the green or the black?"

"Do you want regular delivery or the overnight delivery?"

"Would an appointment Tuesday morning be okay or would you prefer Wednesday afternoon?"

Your Choice Close(s):

_____

_____

Assume-the-Sale Close

"How many should I send out this time, Mr. _____ ?"
"I'll stop by Thursday around 10:00 A.M., okay?"

Your Assume-the-Sale Close(s):

_____

_____

12

Service Will Make
or Break You

I've mentioned before that I was in the security alarm industry for many years. We focused our efforts on large commercial accounts. This is not to say we didn't sell a lot of residential security systems and small businesses. We certainly did. They came to us by virtue of the excellent reputation we worked very hard to build in our community. However, our daily sales focus was always the major accounts. Our feelings were that nearly every time, the customer was king and deserved to be treated just as we would want someone to treat us. I say "nearly every time" because we also experienced some rough business dealings with people who had every intention of taking advantage of us. Fortunately these people are few and far between. Most business firms, large and small, are honorable and deserve to be treated as such unless proven otherwise.

TECHNIQUES OF SELLING AGAINST YOUR LARGE COMPETITORS

When you sell large accounts you will always have competition nipping at your heels. Many people realize the profitability of selling major accounts. Most times, in order to get business we would have to submit bids or proposals, which then would be compared against those submitted by our competitors.

Some of the firms bidding against us would be large, national corporations. Sometimes, simply because of their national reputation and little else, we'd lose a bid to those people. The buyers felt safe using them.

SELLING AGAINST THE LOWBALL PRICE CUTTERS

Some of the firms bidding against us would be smaller and relatively new in the business—firms known in the industry as lowballers. That means their bids would be unbelievably cheap, occasionally cheaper than I could do the job at my wholesale cost. When a firm does that, it's called "buying the business."

Why would sane people sell below cost? Some believed that to do so would get them started selling a major account and they would make it up on future business. Others wanted to have the major account on their customer list to impress other potential accounts. A few were such bad businesspeople they didn't know they'd lose money. While I would offer my very best price to major accounts, I never did so at the first price quote. I'd want to be positive they would order enough to make it worthwhile. I always avoided selling below cost.

Nearly all buyers in large corporations are well trained in dealing with vendors. While it is their job to obtain the best prices possible, they recognize that vendors must earn enough profit to stay in business—otherwise the buyers are always running around finding new suppliers, which is a big drain on their time. They also know the general value of what they are buying. An unusually low price is often a warning signal to buyers that the bidder doesn't know what he or she is doing.

When faced with prices I couldn't underbid or national competitors who were obviously much larger, I'd always work the service angle. Sometimes if I felt sweetening the deal would help, instead of cutting price I'd extend the guarantee or warranty period. I'd also make sure they knew how great our service and delivery was.

Remember the section on testimonial letters back in Chapter 6 on sales presentations? This is one of several occasions where those little babies have a lot of clout. I'd try to have with me a few testimonial letters from customers about how excellent our service was. I knew that one thing most buyers in large firms really fear is buying something that later creates a big problem for the company. I also knew that most salespeople are too lazy to obtain and carry around testimonial letters as I did.

Did this get me business every time? Certainly not. Some buyers are so focused on low price that nothing else counts. They just don't hear you. If I didn't sell at that point, I'd follow up every six months to see what was happening and remind the buyer of our great service. In many (not all) cases the buyer would have discovered by then what I already knew about this kind of competition.

THE MYTH OF GOOD SERVICE

First, large corporations that compete with you rarely can give as good service as smaller ones. This isn't on purpose. In fact, they may have employees who work very hard to give good service. Their weakness lies in their strongest feature, their large size. As companies grow in size, they must add departments, managers, new paperwork, regulations, policies, and so on. Even if their company was built upon excellent service, as they grow they attract some employees who couldn't care less, who are there simply for a paycheck and the benefit package.

Over time, even if top management wants to provide excellent service, they just can't do so on a consistent basis at the customer-service level. There are a few major corporations in this country that can and do provide excellent customer service, but the truth is they are the exception, not the rule.

Second, what about the "cheapest prices in town" guys? They usually go one of two ways. They either raise their prices or, over a period of time, get so deeply in debt they go out of business. For these firms, service is just a word.

They are not making much profit, if any at all, from sales, yet the daily cost of operating the business continues. Cash flow is their enemy. They are always looking for more business to keep cash in the checking account. They wind up paying their bills late, so pressure from creditors keeps them focused on just one thing: selling new business.

To provide excellent service you must make an investment of people, equipment, and time—all of which cost money. The "cheapest guy in town" simply can't provide it. In the first place, he or she doesn't have any money available to tie up in service. In the second place, this person is so stressed to keep selling new business that he or she can't afford the time to worry about old customers. That's why his or her promises are just that—promises, but ones that can't be kept.

I want you, as a small businessperson, to understand that you need not be the cheapest bidder nor the largest bidder to sell good business accounts or, if you sell to consumers, to sell a wealthier clientele. You must, however, have a commitment for good cus-

---

TED'S #1 RULE

If you don't take care of
your customers,
someone else will.

---

tomer service and keep all the promises you make to customers.

Your toughest competition in most selling situations will be businesspeople just like you who have also decided to make a commitment to good customer service.

ACKNOWLEDGING ORDERS

One area some small businesspeople forget is paperwork. None of us really like it, yet to succeed, a certain amount is mandatory.

One necessary document is a sales agreement. Anyone in direct sales should have a sales agreement that outlines exactly what is being sold to the customer, how the customer will receive it, how it is to be paid for, and whatever terms and conditions you do business on. Without question, an attorney should be consulted as to proper wording. It should be filled out completely, signed by the buyer and the salesperson at the time the order is placed, and the customer given a legible copy.

Problems arise after salespeople leave a sale unless every detail is put in writing. People often don't remember what was said, and you can quickly lose very good customers over issues such as delivery or installation dates and when payment is due.

By handing your new customer a written agreement with all the details covered and his or her signature agreeing to it you have just saved yourself a multitude of misunderstandings.

HOW TO AVOID LOSING CUSTOMERS OVER MONEY OR DELIVERY

I used to make getting a sales contract signed look like I was simply performing good customer service. It took the pressure off asking someone to sign a legal document and give me a check. Here's what I'd say once the sale was closed:

"Ms. _____ , just let me write down all these details so we don't make any mistakes later on." (*At this point I'd fill out the sales contract. I'd then walk over to the new customer's side, set the contract down where we both could view it, and point to the highlights with my pen tip.*)

"Here's what I've got Ms. _____. We'll be installing a _____ (*I always got very detailed so when the price was mentioned the customer was fully aware of what value he or she was getting*). The installation date will be during the week of the twenty-fifth of this month. Your warranty includes _____ . Your total investment for all of this is only $ _____ . That includes the initial investment of $ _____ , for which you'll give me a check today, and the balance will be payable upon your satisfaction with the completed installation. You'll just give a check to our installer when he's done. Does that cover everything?"

If the new customer agreed I'd simply say, "Good, just give me your okay on the paperwork and I'll get this entered immediately." Occasionally the customer will point out something you forgot or something extra he or she wants. Whatever it is, this is the very best time to work it out, while you're there with the buyer. When you close a sale like this, it's very rare to have a cancellation or disagreement later on. In addition, the customer sees that you are concerned with living up to your part of the bargain.

WHAT IF YOU CAN'T KEEP YOUR PROMISE?

Here's where some people make a big mistake. They promise something to get an order, then find out it can't be done. Fearing a cancellation, they hide the fact from the customer, who finds out much later, or they have someone else deliver the bad news. The customer goes nuts and either causes a big uproar with management and/or cancels the order, vowing never to do business with your company again and bad-mouthing you to other potential customers.

How much simpler life can be when, faced with such a situation, you deal with it squarely. It's always best for the person who sells the order to handle the bad news also. He or she is the one the customer knows best and feels most comfortable with at that point.

If it's a missed delivery or installation date, a price increase, or some other major issue, consider it a 50/50 chance the customer will get upset. In other words, half the customers are so busy with something else they will accept your explanation and tell you it's okay, just go ahead.

The other half will get upset, some will even yell, and a few will threaten to cancel. A smart strategy is to let them do some complaining, even yelling, with very little interruption from you other than, "I can appreciate how you might feel." While it may sound upsetting for a few minutes, nearly all people will calm down *if* you first let them vent their feelings.

Don't keep interrupting with excuses or arguments. Allow them to express how they feel. What you must never do is act like it's somehow their fault and try to find something to put the blame on them. Don't patronize them or trade nasty, snide little remarks. Don't tell them it's nothing to get upset about—they *are* upset. Treat them exactly the way you would want someone to treat you with a serious complaint.

As they calm down, continue your explanation, tell them it's not how you normally do business, and be sure they know how very sorry you and your company are. Tell them you'd like to continue in any event. One strategy is, after they calm down, to offer them a little something extra, nothing major because that looks like a bribe, just something to let them know you acknowledge their inconvenience and want to make amends.

We used to give an extended six-month service warranty instead of the standard three-month that came standard. If you sell a product, perhaps give some additional product at no charge or samples of something they didn't order but might enjoy. A few times I gave a gift certificate for two to a nice restaurant. It isn't really what you give them as much as the fact they see you care enough about them to make things right. So few companies think like this that you stand out.

Rarely will people actually cancel *if* they see you make a sincere effort to treat them fairly. But what if they do cancel? Then let them and do it with a smile. Don't threaten to sue, don't point out they are being jerks, don't part ways angry, with insults flying. Be a real man or woman about it by agreeing you disagree and part ways with a handshake. The world is smaller than you think and you don't need unnecessary enemies telling others what a bad outfit you are. You may very well meet again under different circumstances.

COLLECTING MONEY

One of the toughest problems for a small business is cash flow—keeping enough cash available to meet payroll, buy necessary supplies, and pay bills. There is a balance to keep between what you sell and how fast you can get paid. If you sell too much too quickly, you won't have the money to fill the orders. If you sell too slowly, you'll use up your small profits on overhead and not be able to fill future orders when they come in.

Some businesspeople tend not to pay a lot of attention to their accounts receivable unless they get into a crisis situation, then find they can't collect as fast as they thought they could. They also will extend credit much too freely, often to people who really don't deserve it.

I found from hard experience that just because someone has a business does not make him or her creditworthy. When I was first starting out in business, one afternoon, out of sheer financial desperation, I found that when you make a sale, if you ask, many companies, including large ones, can and will cut you a check for a down payment on the spot—but only if you ask. Here's how I used to ask for a check:

I'd wait until I'd made the sale, then as I got out the paperwork I'd say, "Mr. _____, your total investment will be $ _____ . Our normal business terms are a check for half down today with the order and the balance payable upon the satisfactory completion of the installation. You can just give the check to our installer."

"But we use a purchase order system. I was going to issue you one today," the customer might respond.

I'd say, "Well, in that case I'd need three credit references and a bank reference. I must tell you it will delay the order a few weeks for the paperwork to be processed. Just to save time and inconvenience, is there any way you might be able to do it the other way today?"

Notice I never really refused, just made it hard to do, and asked again for a check. In some very large companies and in all government sales, it's either take a purchase order or no sale. However, my real-life experience, over many years, is that the vast majority of companies I sold could and would write a check as requested. Even when I was told they only could buy if I took a purchase order, I never, ever lost a single sale by asking.

Some small businesspeople feel it's embarrassing or demeaning to ask. They feel it makes them look small in the eyes of the buyer. Nonsense! Just act like it's company policy and you do it every time. People don't know differently and frankly, don't care. The key is, you can double your cash flow by collecting as you go instead of billing. I promise you, many other large and small companies have examined their credit policies and do the very same thing.

If you do take a purchase order, always ask for three credit references and get all this information on each: company name, name of person they do business with, business address, city, state, zip code, area code and telephone number; how long they have had credit there, the largest amount of credit they have charged, and what products or services the company sells.

It's a bad sign if they give you public utilities as credit references (they are not acceptable), if they are vague about the names and addresses, or if they start to get upset. Remember, you don't owe anyone credit and any legitimate business with a line of credit will understand your request and not give you a hard time about it. You need then to verify, by telephone, the credit references.

CUSTOMERS YOU CAN LIVE WITHOUT

The groups I'm about to describe are fortunately fairly rare in business. Most people you do business with will be no problem, or problems you can work out. From time to time, however, you'll find some really difficult people who can cost you not only money, but a lot of time and aggravation. Some people become so difficult to do business with that by the time you are finished, you have lost, not gained.

One problem group is people who demand credit unreasonably. No business is obligated to extend credit. It's a privilege, not a right. Be willing to walk away from unreasonable situations.

Some people must be chased for money owed. I remember one guy where I had to actually get in my car, drive over to his place, and demand a check or I would never have collected. If you are desperate for business it's hard to throw away any customer, but are you really making any profit on people who require this much of your time?

Some people are chronic complainers. No matter what you do, something doesn't satisfy them. I'm a firm believer in good customer service, but when you receive repeated complaints from one person or company you need to identify what's going on. If you are at fault then correct the problem, at your expense. On the other hand, if the complaints are vague or about uncorrectable situations, then you may be dealing with a chronic complainer. You must make a decision as to when you will tell them that's all you can do. This is a very important reason to have a written sales agreement between yourself and the customer, spelling out exactly what you agree to do.

I recall a few times over the years when we just gave people their money back and considered ourselves lucky to be out of the situation. One complainer, an elderly gentlemen, was such a pain I gave him all his money back and let him keep the security system, fearing if I sent someone to remove it he'd claim something was damaged during the removal. Three weeks later he called to complain one of the buttons on the system was sticking and was trying to demand a free service call!

Another problem account is where price is king. These people buy from the cheapest vendor they can find. You can spend a lot of time showing them why paying a little more is going to give them a lot more in product and service. They pretend to listen, then buy the cheapest. They'll drag in vendors with promises of more profitable opportunities "in the future."

I've found that these price buyers are also the most insistent when it comes to demanding extras, such as faster-than-average delivery and better-than-average warranties. They are very demanding about quality and performance once the sale is completed. If something doesn't work, they often insist you take it back, not fix it as you normally would.

In other words, they want every possible advantage and to pay next to nothing for it. Small businesspeople get these frequently because price buyers know they are not as sophisticated as the larger firms who won't give in to their strong-arm tactics.

There's no law that says people must pay your price. I've negotiated many a deal over the years, some profitable, some I really made very little money. I expect that it's part of being in business. However, if you have customers you never can make a profit on, time after time, then consider seriously dropping them and spending that time looking for more profitable business.

HERE ARE SECRETS OF GETTING NEW CUSTOMERS FROM PRESENT CUSTOMERS

1. We used to let our existing customer base know they would receive some free service if they would recommend someone who became a customer.

2. Whenever I hired a new salesperson I'd have him or her call all our old customers whom we had not sold for a very long time, or had lost for some reason, to see if they'd like to consider doing business with us again.

3. We'd mail out reward posters that said in part "Wanted: new customer, must need security system. Reward: one month's free service." It was another way to remind our customers of our offer.

4. Every time we added new products or services I'd have my salespeople get on the phone to every existing customer we had. It's always less costly and easier to sell an existing customer a new service than to turn up a new prospect from scratch.

13

Goals: Time Management's Twin

I can't complete any book on sales without discussing personal motivation, goal setting, and effective time management. If you're not a good manager of your time, you can't be a good businessperson, let alone salesperson. More importantly, since you'll be responsible for both sales and running a business, you must have a daily focus on what is important and to what degree is it important in relationship to the whole picture.

PERSONAL MOTIVATION

Much has been written about motivating people. Many people, often sales managers who should really know better, confuse motivation with excitement. Heck, it's not hard to get someone all excited. Just walk outdoors, find a stranger, and throw a bucket of water on him or her. You'll see excitement.

Many people contact me to motivate their sales staff. What they really hope I'll do is get the salespeople so riled up they'll go out and sell twice what they usually sell. I always feel bad for them when I explain what motivation is, and is not. It isn't excitement, not often anyway. It's not ranting, raving motivational speakers or brass bands or company songs—not even monster prizes offered for sales improvement. I know people use these strategies every day. I also know they work—for a short time. The problem is, it's *only* a short time. Unfortunately when they wear off, the motivated people get lower than they were before.

179

So what does motivate people? What will motivate you every day to succeed? The answer is deep inside each of us. It comes from knowing what you want to do, what it takes to get it done, and how you plan to do it—in short, having goals that mean something to you and a workable plan for their achievement.

Some of the most motivated and dedicated people I've ever had the privilege of meeting (and I always feel privileged to meet people like that) are very calm people. They don't need to be stimulated to the point of jumping up and down with a group of screaming people at a pep rally.

I have nothing against reading or listening to personal motivation speakers; I've often done it myself. For many years I had a commute to work of nearly an hour each way. I believe I profited greatly by listening to cassette tapes from some of the great masters of selling, marketing, psychology, and business as well as motivational tapes.

The key phrase is profit. I wasn't listening to people trying to get me all excited. Instead, they were sharing ideas I could put to use in my daily life. I have always found learning new ideas and ways to accomplish worthwhile goals stimulating and highly motivating.

Two (of many) audio programs I recall as I write this were Dr. Norman Vincent Peal and Dr. Robert Schuller. Not only did they motivate me, they educated me. I read Dale Carnegie's book, *How to Win Friends and Influence People*, 20-some years ago. To this day I remember and practice some of Mr. Carnegie's suggestions for getting along with and working with people. He wrote this book in 1936 and I understand it's sold over 15 million copies. The truth of what he wrote is so powerful, so true, that you can still buy a new paperback copy at most large book vendors. Imagine, 60-some years later and people are still eager to buy the book in quantities large enough to justify publication!

What I am illustrating for you is that knowledge is power. You can achieve any worthwhile goal by following the rules set forth in this chapter. If you focus on what's important to you, then focus on obtaining it, you'll be motivated. Every time you learn a new skill that takes you closer to your goals your motivation will increase. The secret to motivation is what's important to you.

After you finish this book, go to your library or bookseller and look up the three authors I mentioned above. If selling makes you a little uncomfortable, as we discussed in earlier chapters, then see what these authors have to say on the topics of assertiveness and self-esteem.

GOAL SETTING FIRST, TIME MANAGEMENT SECOND

Before I discuss time management in the following chapter, I must explain goal setting. The two go together. Before you can practice good time management, you must first examine your goals carefully. You need to know what's important and in what priority. Only then can time management really help you.

GOALS...

The greatest danger for most of us

is not that our aim is too high and we miss it,

but that our aim is too low and we reach it.

Some people may get a little uncomfortable with this. You started out reading about how to sell in your business and suddenly the author's asking you to make major decisions about your life. Please, don't skip this valuable chapter. I won't force you to do anything. I will share some very important ideas that I know will aid you as you walk the long road to success. In fact, I know some shortcuts. Please read on.

Have you ever wondered why so many people fail or just struggle along in life, while others succeed? Have you ever really spent any time to find out why some people seem to do well while others barely survive or simply don't make it at all? (I'm not talking about just business efforts, I'm talking about life.) If you did, you'd see very quickly that the people who are doing well, for the most part, are very goal oriented. This goal-oriented attitude leads them to be time conscious. They know what they must do, so they make sure they have enough time to do it. They spend their time effectively because they have a reason to do so.

The majority of people have few, if any, goals that will help them through life. They simply live and respond to the moment. They spend five days a week, eight hours a day working, and the rest of their time goes to whatever looks interesting at the moment.

It's not that they are incapable of success. It's not that they are lazy (well, some are). It's not that they don't have talent, and it's certainly not because they are not nice people—most are very nice people. It's just that they don't want success bad enough to spend time planning it and working toward it.

If you ask what their goals are, they have a combination of high-sounding, vague ideas, hopes, and daydreams. Nothing specific. Nothing you can measure in terms of achievement. Their goals in life are so vague that if they ever did achieve them they probably wouldn't recognize them.

"I want to be rich" or "I want to be a success" or "I want a new home" or "I want to meet someone special." Nice goals you think?

What the heck do any of them mean? Just how rich is rich? A success, what is your version of success, would you know? A new home? Where, how big, what does it look like? What neighborhood will it be in? Meet someone special would you? I happen to know a criminal psychiatrist who studies serial killers; he knows some really "special" people, how about a blind date?

Sound pretty silly? The point is, it's no sillier than the goals of most people today who walk around in a fog, waiting to hit the lottery so they can get on with their life. And what if they don't hit the lottery? Well, they don't want to think about that. Just keep a positive thought and hope for the best. Gotta go now.

Being a salesperson is a tough way to earn a living. Owning a business and being its salesperson is even tougher. Yet I can tell you now that some of this country's most successful people, including top executives in major corporations and highly successful entrepreneurs, started their careers as salespeople.

You do not have to be a salesperson to take advantage of good selling skills. Often, in both your personal and business life, the skills you learn as a salesperson will give you an advantage over people with no such skills. Selling is no more than understanding human behavior and working with it to achieve goals. Having goals is the key.

My Sailing Ship Analogy

Picture for a moment this scene: a warm, bright sunny afternoon by the ocean. You and I are standing on the pier, observing a lovely sailing ship as it hoists anchor. The sailors on board open the beautiful white sails, the soft summer breeze begins to fill them, and the boat slowly moves forward. But we have a small problem. The ship has no rudder with which to guide it. The sailors have removed it.

My question to you is, where will the ship go? Will it slowly allow the wind to take it out to sea? Will it simply go back and forth in the harbor, hitting against the harbor walls and going nowhere? If it does go to sea, will it find a safe port before it runs out of supplies for the sailors on board or will it just wind up on some beach someplace? Or will it drift at sea forever, until it finally sinks for one reason or another?

Who knows? You don't know, do you? The sailors on the ship don't know. I certainly don't know. Nobody has a clue. In this analogy, the ship represents a person, starting out in great shape, with lots of hope and dozens of great but somewhat vague ideas—but no specific goals.

Just as a ship in real life would, after being at sea a long time, you deteriorate as time goes by. We all do, it's called aging. As we get older, we start slowing down, we start to become a little more pessimistic. Our ideas slowly become less grand. If we started out in life with few or no goals, or if our goals were not realistic but more of a daydream, as we get older, living without specific goals becomes a way of life.

As we reach retirement age we grow bitter and angry because all our dreams disappeared, unfulfilled. They slipped away so slowly we didn't even see them going. We allowed the trivial little aspects of life to fill our lives so completely we never had time.

Sad? Depressing? You better believe it. It's a waste of otherwise good people who, in most cases, could turn their lives around if they would just focus on what's really important to them.

Some Good News

Understand that this situation is never, ever cast in stone. At any time in your life, even after retirement, you can reverse this, *if you want to.* The decision to sail around in a boat without a rudder *is a choice*, just as it's anyone's choice not to have goals. No one can stop you from having positive goals and acting on them *unless you allow it.*

One of the big reasons I really enjoy teaching sales and small business courses is that some of my students are people who have made a conscious effort to make a positive change in their lives. I really respect that.

I have respect for you also. You either looked this book up in a library or purchased it in order to enhance your life. (If by some chance you stole this book, you rascal, I take this last sentence back. On the other hand, if you return this book, then I won't take the last sentence back and I'll respect you. Choices—we always have choices.)

A Little Story You'll Enjoy

I want to share a story about one of my students. We'll call him Jack, not his real name. Jack was recently retired when he entered my sales class. He had a real sales personality and I told him so after class one evening. When he said he had never sold anything in his life I was quite surprised. He explained he'd been a purchasing agent in a factory for over 40 years. His job when he retired was in essence the same as when he had started. I had an impression he had not earned or saved very much money. He said he was looking for something part time.

As we talked, Jack told me how he had envied the salespeople calling on him when he was a purchasing agent. "It looked like such an interesting way to earn a living, almost all of them seemed to be happy with their job. Not like me, hating it every day for 40-some years. I always wished I could have started selling when I was younger, I could have made some decent money."

I asked him why he had not done so all those years ago. "Well, you know, a wife, then kids came along. I was afraid to rock the boat," he said. "What about after the kids grew up?" I asked. "Well, my wife and I talked about it. She thought it was a good idea, but, well, you know how it is. I never got around to making the move. Maybe I was a little scared. Then my wife passed away three years ago and I decided to stick it out for the pension. Unfortunately, the pension doesn't go very far these days. I need a job for some pocket change, maybe as a salesclerk or something like that. I decided to see what your class in selling was about."

"Jack," I responded, "I'm going to ask you a favor. I want you to fill out these goal-setting sheets and bring them to class next time. You have nothing to lose so I want your promise that you'll keep an open mind and fill them out honestly. No one but you and I will ever see them. After class next week, we'll review them."

I did nothing to influence Jack nor did I tell him where to seek out employment. I just made sure he was honest with himself about what he wanted for the rest of his life. For Jack, being true with himself and acknowledging what he really wanted, not worrying about what someone else might say, was a big struggle. I remember he rewrote his goals at least three times before he felt he was being genuine with his own needs. After his last sales class, I didn't see him again. The last thing he told me was he was interviewing with a few local companies.

About three years later, I was going to my car after shopping in a local mall when I heard a familiar voice. "Mr. Tate, Mr. Tate. How are you?" It was Jack, walking along with a very attractive lady about his age. He was beaming.

He told me after leaving class he surprised himself by turning down two part-time sales jobs because they "didn't fit my goals." He accepted a trial arrangement with a local real-estate firm. "The minute I started, I liked it. Every morning I was actually looking forward to the day. My friends tried to warn me I couldn't pass the state license exam at my age. They said it would be too difficult. They said I was too old. They were wrong, it was easy. I really enjoyed studying for it. I should have done this years ago," Jack explained. "I'm earning more money part time now than I did full time."

He introduced me to the lady he was with. It turned out to be his second wife. He told me how she came in one day about selling her house because she had been widowed recently. Before she left the office, Jack not only had secured her real-estate listing, but also a dinner date that Saturday night. As we parted that evening in the parking lot I watched Jack escort his wife to a brand-new Lincoln. "I've decided to get a new one each year, sort of make up for all those years of driving cars until they fell apart," he told me as he left.

Taking Responsibility

Did I do that? Absolutely not. I had very little to do with Jack's overwhelming success. Other than teaching him in the regular sales-class training he had signed up for, all I did was encourage Jack to be truthful *to himself* about his personal goals. I've done that with many people who, for reasons only they know, can't do it by themselves. Their lives never change, they just go on, hoping, but they never take action.

Every good thing after that was based on Jack's personal efforts, Jack's willingness to take personal responsibility for his life and get on with it was really important *to him*. He didn't let other people tell him what was important to him, he knew. More importantly, he had the courage to stay with his goals. He did it. You can do it. I don't care how old or young you are. The great part about goal setting is, it's never too late. You can change things for the better whenever you decide to make a serious effort. No one is standing in your way except you.

A Personal Story Regarding Perseverance

When I was 17 I enrolled in a mail-order course to learn the art of writing. My writing tool was an old black Smith-Corona typewriter, the kind you see in old movies from the '30s and '40s. I took several lessons and started to write a book idea. I also wrote a couple of articles for magazines and submitted one of them.

Nobody encouraged me and in fact I had the feeling my dad felt I was wasting my time, although he never said that to me. The article I submitted was rejected. I allowed myself to start believing I was wasting my time and I quit.

Over the course of many years and several careers, I did write—advertising, public-relations copy, articles for trade publications, all sorts of things. I did it successfully. I just never thought of myself as a writer. I just thought of it as part of a job.

Many years later, more than I care to admit, I was going through an old box of papers. It was my old writing course and the things I had written, in failure, all those many years ago.

As I started to read the material I realized it was pretty good for a 17-year-old kid. It was crude in spots, but nothing a little editing couldn't fix. It dawned on me as I sat there reading I had never failed as a writer.

I hadn't taken the time to really learn the craft before I started submitting articles. I was trying to rush the process and when it didn't work the first time, I quit. I allowed my dad's silent disapproval plus my own impatience to cut off what could have been a lifetime of writing.

Looking back, I'm not really sure about my dad's silent disapproval. He never said anything negative or positive. I just read between the lines. I never discussed it with him, which I really should have. I was afraid he might disapprove if I did. So as you can see, I made a major decision in my life based upon trying to read someone's mind and one rejection!

That's how a lot of people make decisions. The minute the going gets tough, they back down. They don't have enough self-confidence to see something through.

Many years in business and selling have taught me to be my own person. To trust my gut feelings. To stay the course. If something in your life is important enough to you to be a serious goal, then recognize from the very beginning there will be ups and downs. The world is filled with negative people who see nothing but the bad side of everything.

If you want something badly and it makes sense to you, then have the courage to go for it.

WHAT DO YOU REALLY WANT?

Why are you reading this book? Please don't get vague. If I hear someone say one more time, "To better myself" or "To get a better understanding of sales" or "Just to see what's out there" I think I'll scream.

Be honest. When you lie to yourself you are only cheating one person. Tell the raw truth, "My business is in trouble, we are not selling what we should" or "My boss is going to fire me if my sales don't pick up" or "I hate my job and I'm thinking about starting up a business of my own" or "I need to earn more money, maybe something in this book will help." Now these are a few of several real reasons someone might want to read a good book on small business selling.

Whatever reason caused you to read this book is very possibly connected to your personal and/or business goals. As you continue to read, give thought to what's important to you—not to your spouse, kids, family, friends, neighbors, co-workers—just you. We'll come back to this shortly. For now, just give it some thought.

WHY DOESN'T EVERYONE HAVE GOALS?

What do you think about when you wake up on a workday? Do you hate to think about it? Do you have a problem getting started for work on Monday mornings?

Ever hear the saying, "You become what you think about?" It's true. Start out the day with negative thoughts on the way to work and the day will go that way. Start out the day feeling good about getting into the job and you'll spend a rewarding day.

Now I can't change how you feel about your job or anything else, but if your daily life routine is bad news, you have the power to make a change for the better. Does it take courage? Certainly it does. Is there a price to pay? Almost always. Is it scary? It can be. At best, change is often uncomfortable, at least in the beginning. Is it hard work? Yes, at times it can be.

For many people, these and a few other basic reasons are enough not to move forward in their lives. If you decide to maintain the status quo, you'll be in the majority. Very few people have the courage to really set goals and work at them for any period of time. That's one very good reason why successful people in our society stand out and reap such great rewards: There are so few of them! (The 80–20 rule, remember?)

WHAT GOALS WILL DO FOR YOU

If you do establish goals, realistic ones that have a true meaning to you, you'll put yourself onto the fast track for success—if that's one of your goals. When you have goals for various aspects of your business and personal life, it's surprising how things fall into place. You will have little trouble deciding what to do every day when you awake. You'll know immediately. When situations arise where there is doubt as to what to do, your predetermined goals will help you decide, decisively.

Some people think success is hard, too hard for them. Without goals it is. Success isn't hard *if* you know what you want and develop a plan to get it. Goals get you through.

I placed this chapter before the one on time management because successful time management rarely works unless motivated by goals, your goals.

TED'S NINE RULES FOR SUCCESSFUL GOALS

1. The goal must be something that has real meaning to you.
2. The goal must be obtainable.
3. The goal must be measurable.
4. The goal must be specific.
5. The goal must have a timetable set for its achievement.
6. The goal needs a priority set for it in relation to your other goals.
7. Larger, more difficult goals should be broken down into a series of smaller goals.
8. Long- and medium-range goals are important, but focus hardest on what you can do in the next 90 days.
9. To maintain a healthy life you need goals for all areas, both personal and business.

Rules for Successful Goals

1. *The goal must be something that has real meaning to you.* Otherwise you won't stay with it very long, no matter how well meaning you are. That's why you need to set goals by yourself, not let others talk you into goals that they think you need.

2. *The goal must be obtainable.* Setting unrealistic goals you'll never have a real chance to obtain is depressing and counterproductive.

3. *The goal must be measurable.* "I want to be rich" can't be measured. "I want to have $10,000 in my savings account" can be.

4. *The goal must be specific.* "I want to be happy" doesn't define what happy means. However, if a vacation to Europe would make you happy, then your goal would be, "I want to take a vacation to Europe."

5. *The goal must have a timetable set for its achievement.* That means a specific date as to when this goal will happen. Otherwise the goal is meaningless.

6. *The goal needs a priority set for it in relation to your other goals.* Rating goals, on a scale of 1 to 5 or 1 to 10 helps you to know immediately what action to take when the goals conflict. Not every goal is as important as another.

7. *Larger, more difficult goals should be broken down into a series of smaller goals.* "I want $250,000 in a retirement account" is not something most people can do anything about except wish. If you have 20 years to retirement you could decide to save $12,500 per year. To make it more realistic you would make your goal to bank $241 per week for the next 20 years. If you would find $241 a week is not realistic, then reset the goal for something that is.

8. *To maintain a healthy life you need goals for all areas of your life, both business and personal.* All work or all play is not good. Life should be a balance.

9. *Never be afraid to reevaluate your goals.* As we grow in life, we reach certain goals and no longer need to keep them on our list. Our personal and business needs and attitudes change.

New people come into our lives, others leave. From time to time it's important to sit down and take a long look at all our goals, changing them or giving them new priorities as needed.

The Five Major Areas of Goal Setting

1. *Business and sales goals.* Develop goals daily, monthly, and yearly. For instance, if you sell you may have a certain number of new accounts as your goal or perhaps a certain dollar volume.

2. *Financial goals.* Planning your income now for your future is just smart thinking. Set up savings and goals for retirement, kids' education, insurance, buying a home, or whatever is important in your personal life. If you have a personal computer there are several excellent computer programs that can help.

3. *Family/social goals.* If you are young and single your goals may go toward meeting a potential mate or going out with your friends regularly. Married people may want goals related to good relationships such as finding time for doing social things with their spouse or perhaps finding quality time with their children.

4. *Spiritual goals.* Depending upon your personal beliefs, finding time on a regular basis to get in touch with this aspect of your life can be a very rewarding and refreshing goal.

5. *Personal-growth goals.* Continue to educate yourself. Never allow yourself to become stagnant. Reading good books that will contribute to your business success (like this little baby you're now reading), listening to audio tapes, taking seminars and workshops, associating with your peers, all make excellent goals.

THE EASY WAY TO SET GOALS

I've been involved in classroom situations, as a student, where I was asked to set my goals. I frequently had a problem doing so. It was very hard for me in my younger days to see 30 years down the road. For instance, some people were putting down things like buy a home and save for the kids' college education. At that time I wasn't even married, let alone have kids. I knew these were very worthy goals and someday I may want them, but not then. Hell, my goal that week was to dig up a date for the weekend who could chew gum and walk at the same time.

I just wasn't all that sure. I felt like something was wrong with me. It wasn't until much later that I learned many people have the same difficulty. An instructor showed me some ideas that eliminated the pressure of making quick life decisions I was uncertain about, but allowed me to set realistic goals that would move me in a positive direction where I could then decide the long-term ones.

Here's how: First, decide your goals for the next five years and tackle the longer-term ones, such as saving for retirement and so on, at a later time. You need three sheets of blank paper to copy the examples shown. Write at the top of each, Five-Year Goals (Figure 13.1), One-Year Goals (Figure 13.2), 90-Day Goals (Figure 13.3).

Start with the Five-Year Goals. Think about how and where you'd like to be in five years. For instance, how will your business be doing then? Will you have other salespeople, perhaps a sales manager working for you then? How many other employees? What kind of dollar volume will you gross?

Do the same for Personal, Family/Social, Spiritual, and Financial goals. What would you honestly like to see in your life then?

Next, fill in your One-Year Goals. What would you like to achieve over the next year? You may have other goals here that can be accomplished in a year or less. For some of the answers, look at your Five-Year Goals and divide what it takes to accomplish by five.

For instance, let's say a Five-Year Goal is to buy a new home. You know from shopping around you'll need a $30,000 cash down payment for the kind of home you want. Divide that by five and you'll get $6,000, which is the amount you'll need to save annually for the next five years to buy your home. A One-Year Goal then becomes to save $6,000 over the next 12 months.

Next, fill in the 90-Day Goals. You need to save $6,000 over a year, and there are four 90-day periods in a year. Dividing four into $6,000 equals $1,500 you need to save every 90 days. That's still not

Five-year goal planner for: _____	
From _____ 19 ____ To _____ 19 ____	
Sales Goals	
Personal Growth	
Family/Social	
Spiritual Goals	
Financial Goals	

Figure 13.1 My personal five-year goal worksheet.

One-year goal planner for: _____	
From _____ 19 ____ To _____ 19 ____	
Sales Goals	
Personal Growth	
Family/Social	
Spiritual Goals	
Financial Goals	

Figure 13.2 My personal one-year goal worksheet.

90-day goal planner for: _____	
From _____ **19** ____ **To** _____ **19** ____	
Sales Goals	
Personal Growth	
Family/Social	
Spiritual Goals	
Financial Goals	

Figure 13.3 My personal 90-day goal worksheet.

specific enough. If you get a paycheck every week, you need to set the money aside as you receive it, no excuses. So divide the year's needed savings ($6,000) by the number of weeks in a year (52) and you'll get $115.39 as the amount to save out of every weekly paycheck.

When you work this process out for your bigger goals in life, there can be several different results.

First, take a long look at what's required to achieve the goal and decide if it's worth the effort. Perhaps a goal only *sounds* good.

Second, using the house down payment as an example, you realize you simply can't afford to save that much every week. Here you'd have choices. One choice is to set aside an amount you can realistically afford and set your goals on a lower-priced home with a lower down payment. Or, you could also decide simply not to do it. Another choice, perhaps, is to decide you need a better job with higher pay and make that a goal with a higher priority than the house. Third, you may realize you can easily afford this amount and decide to save for an even better home. Or you may just save twice as fast and achieve this goal in two and a half years instead of five.

The point is, when you start to get serious about your life, when you start to determine what's important to you, a great many choices and opportunities arise. Actually, these choices are available now, but you don't see them until you start thinking out your goals and how you can achieve them (see Figure 13.4).

Why Do So Many People Skip This Part?

There are many reasons—here are a few common ones. The goals they profess to have come from someone else: their parent(s), wife, husband, lover, you name it. They are doing or pretending to do something to please someone else. They usually think it's out of love. It isn't, it's out of guilt.

For instance, a dying mother begs her son to be a doctor. He's ambivalent. There are many other things he's secretly thought of doing, but how can he tell his mom? It's her dream. She passes away, he trucks off to medical school. Now if you ask him, he'll say he's doing this out of love and respect for his mom. He's really doing it

90-day goal planner for: _____	
From _____ **19** ___ **To** _____ **19** ___	
Sales Goals	*1. Close at least three new accounts each week.*
	2. Develop four new referral sources.
	3. Sell at least 10 add-on warranty contracts to clients.
	4. Telemarket 20 calls every A.M. for new business.
Personal Growth	*1. Read at least one good book on selling.*
	2. Attend sales seminar.
Family/Social	*1. Take spouse to dinner at least three times.*
	2. Go camping with family over one weekend.
	3. Attend parents' night at each child's school.
Spiritual Goals	*1. Attend religious services every week.*
	2. Volunteer to assist food drive.
Financial Goals	*1. Save 10 percent of net income each payday.*
	2. Pay off MasterCard to zero balance.

Figure 13.4 Examples of 90-day goal setting.

out of guilt. He needs to be the good son. In order to be a good son he sets aside his personal feelings and becomes a doctor. He lessens the guilt. As he practices medicine, many times his mind wanders to what might have been had he had more courage to live his life the way he wanted to. He forces those thoughts from his mind and continues his medical career. He's never considered a great doctor, never makes any valuable discoveries, just plugs along, his heart only half in it.

Have you ever noticed how at a gathering of old people some seem happy and content? They have the ability to enjoy retirement and whatever it may bring. Some seem angry and discontented, even frustrated. Nothing's ever good enough for these people. They are miserable and, deep down, very sad. People excuse them, feeling it's the infirmities of old age with the aches and pains. For some it is. For others, it's knowing their life is pretty much over and they never accomplished what was important to them. All of the "should have's" keep coming to mind. Here is where our doctor example will arrive, tired and bitter and wondering, always wondering.

Earlier in this chapter we discussed setting goals that are important to you. The only goals that really can help you will come from you. You can't do things that are based on the goals of others. Just as you need to respect the lives of people around you, you need to respect your own needs and goals.

Far too many people will try to make their goals fit someone else's need above their own, such as the doctor example. The world is filled with people who feel it is selfish or in some way horrible to do what is important just for them. It isn't horrible or selfish at all to address your own needs. In fact, if you find yourself constantly putting others' needs ahead of your own, know that these are acts of someone with very low self-esteem. As I've mentioned elsewhere in this book, low self-esteem need not be forever unless you allow it to be.

The one great thing about this world is that we always have choices. Sometimes they are easy, other times they take courage, but they are always there for us if we want them. I hope those of you who can see yourself in these pages will always remember my words about choices.

I asked the question, "Why do so many people skip the part of seriously deciding goals for themselves?" The answer is, as you may have realized by now, that it's too painful to deal with for some of us.

There's another big reason people fail to set goals and work toward them. The word is "lazy." They don't think past next week's party. It's called living for today and not worrying or even considering tomorrow. It's one thing to behave like that in high school and college, another to take that attitude with us into our adult years, yet many do.

I'm a big advocate of living in the present; I honestly feel it's the only way any of us can live our lives effectively. Having said that, I also am a big believer in living in the present in positive ways that will help us achieve positive, worthwhile goals. Living for the moment, for today, is not in any way a conflict with having a series of worthwhile goals for our future.

The reason people have trouble following goals very long is that they are so far away. If you plan and put most of your effort into your 90-day goals, you'll have success that can be measured and the short-term success helps keep you working on the long term.

Remember also that goals have a life of their own. Don't be afraid to change the long-term goals if, as you work on them in the short term, you see they are not realistic or that you've changed your mind

Nearly all your efforts must be working on the short-term goals. You can plan for but never live in the future. When the future arrives, it will be today. Therefore, what you do today is the only important thing.

I remember an instructor in school who used to remind the students, "You can't go back and change yesterday. Tomorrow hasn't arrived yet, and when it does, it will be today. Therefore live for the moment, because that's the only real time you can actually take action."

The Power of Setting Priorities

Finally, on all of your goals set a priority. Use whatever system works best for you. I usually suggest assigning a number from one to 10 for each goal on the list—10 meaning your most-important goal, one meaning your least-important goal.

When conflicts arise, as they will, the priority system is a reminder to you as to what's most important to work on first. It also will suggest to you what goals you need to either put off or simply drop.

GOALS WON'T WORK UNLESS YOU REALLY WANT THEM TO

Goal setting takes both time and effort on your part. Understand that just creating these lists, hard as it might be, is only the first step. I've seen many people develop these lists of goals and still fail to make any significant changes in their lives.

What happens? They are not really ready to make a change, although they talk about it and plan for it. Some people create unrealistic goals. Others assign unrealistic priorities, often high priorities to vague goals. There are dozens of ways to sabotage any plan if they want to do that. Then, of course, they can point to the plan and complain about how it didn't work for them.

What they really want to do is continue on as always, without change. Until you decide within yourself that this is something you want to do, it can't work. That's why setting goals by yourself is so critical to success. It's got to be goals set just for you, written by you, from your heart.

Listen to Your Goals: They Are Speaking to You

As you start, over a period of weeks, maybe months, you'll find some of your goals are in big conflict with others. Some of your goals are really just too much trouble to actually do for what you'll get out of them. New goals you had not considered arise and start to push out the earlier ones. It's okay. It's almost guaranteed to happen that way to some extent.

I want you not to fear this but rather look forward to it. What is happening slowly, over a period of time, is an in-depth evaluation of what's really important to you, and of where you really feel you belong in life. It's an awareness that many people never arrive at until they are way too old to do anything about it. Be grateful you are having this opportunity now.

Keep an open mind. No goal is ever cast in stone. Be flexible. Be willing to drop or make less important some goals while you replace them with others. But if this doesn't happen as you continue to follow up on your goals, if you are working on your original list and have a sense of well-being and achievement as you go about your day, then leave it alone. You simply selected well the first time.

14

Time Management

LOSSES FROM WASTED TIME

In order to succeed at selling, especially if you have other business duties besides selling, you must manage your time well to achieve success. We are all busy, but we always seem to find time to do the things that we want to do. It's finding the time to do the things we *ought* to do that is a problem.

I know some people who equate success with being busy, but there is no truth to that. Some of the most powerful men and women in the business world have lots of time available. They have long since mastered the art of time management and delegation.

I fully understand that many readers of this book are running small businesses either by themselves or with very limited help. Don't worry, I'll still show you how to delegate in a one-person business.

Let's explore some ways people commonly waste time.

TIME...

Why is it we always
can find time for the
things we like to do,

yet never have time
to do the things
we have to do?

Burning Up Valuable Energy

1. Excessive duplication of effort
2. Fixing mistakes, doing the same job twice
3. Continued wheel spinning
4. Excessive time socializing on phone, unplanned traveling, and unnecessary meetings

Destroying Their Motivation

1. Spending large amounts of time on useless activities
2. Talking to and trying to sell unqualified prospects
3. Handling the same paperwork over and over
4. Changing priorities often
5. Unclear objectives and goals
6. Keeping busy doing trivial tasks instead of important ones
7. Personal business during working hours
8. Procrastinating doing the necessary tasks

How We Can Lose Golden Opportunities

Doing the wrong things at the wrong times for the wrong reasons with the wrong people!

Spending Lots of Time on Routine and Familiar Tasks

For many people, keeping busy spells success. They run around all day hopping from one trivial task to another, only to complain in the evening they are further behind than when they started. For some salespeople it's often the perfect excuse as to why they have no time to prospect. They are simply too busy.

Being busy means absolutely nothing to your success unless the task takes you closer to your goals. When people learn to emphasize results instead of activities, they then start to move forward. Think carefully about your goals and objectives. How do those trivial tasks add to your effectiveness, to your success? Remember, it's not how much you do that counts, but how much you get done.

If you stop spending so much time on the trivial, you'll have more time to devote to the important sales activities that will bring you closer to your goals. Take a long look at your daily routine tasks and ask, "What would happen if they weren't done at all?" If the answer is nothing, stop doing them.

Delegating When You Work Alone

Try to delegate the tasks that must be done. If you work alone, can you hire someone to do them? If not, can you send the work out, such as have proposals typed by a typing service or copying done by a copy shop?

Remember, spending time organizing prospect lists, filing, making copies, keeping detailed records, rearranging your desk, and all the other trivial tasks only keep you from having time to be a success. Learn how to focus on the activities that will give you the greatest return.

Many small businesspeople feel they can't afford help, so they go it alone. The reality is, you can't afford *not* to get help to whom you can delegate routine tasks. If money is really short, how about part-time help?

There are many good, talented people who would be grateful for part-time work and really appreciate the opportunity and usually work very hard to keep it. Here's a work-force pool many small businesspeople make the huge mistake of passing up.

1. *Retired people.* A lot of retired people get bored just sitting around their homes. Since many live on limited incomes, they are usually happy to find an opportunity where they can contribute something and get paid for it.

2. *Mothers and housewives.* Many women had careers before marriage. Some now have other responsibilities and can't work full time, but they can work part time.

3. *Disabled people.* There are many jobs that can be done by physically challenged people.

I'm not suggesting you just hire anyone who walks in the door. That would be a big mistake. But if you focus on what you need done

I'm positive in most cases you can find people from these groups who are quite capable of doing the work. Some of the best people I have ever worked with were part-timers from these groups. For many of these people the flexible hours and the opportunity to contribute in a worthwhile way are very important.

Common Time Wasters That Sales and Small Businesspeople Commit

1. Not enough time scheduled for prospecting
2. Interruptions, drop-in visitors, distractions, telephone calls
3. Doing-it-yourself; involved in too many detailed, routine tasks
4. Always crises; fire fighting
5. Lack of objectives, deadlines, and priorities
6. Lots of paperwork, reports, reading material
7. Leaving tasks partly done; jumping from task to task
8. Procrastination, indecision, daydreaming
9. Lack of self-discipline
10. Socializing, idle conversation
11. Failure to do first things first
12. Constantly switching priorities

Solutions to Some Common Time Wasters

1. Lack of Priorities

- Have written daily, weekly, and monthly goals.
- Have a to-do list with priorities. Start with the top priority.
- Use a formal planner or calendar system regularly.

2. Paperwork

- Have a specific time set aside each day for paperwork.
- Handle each piece of paper on your desk only once. Once you pick it up, pretend it has glue on it until you can answer the

question, "What's the next step to do with this?" If you can handle the next step within five minutes, do it immediately. Often there is no next step and you now have a candidate for the wastebasket or at least the filing cabinet. (National statistics show that once something is filed, there is an 80 to 90 percent chance it is never looked at again until it is thrown away.)

3. Meetings

- Don't hold meetings if you can achieve the same results without them.
- Set objectives and agendas and stick with them.
- Have only the right people in attendance.
- Set time limits for meetings and keep them.

4. Being Overwhelmed

- Be able to say "no."
- Eliminate lower-priority items from your schedule.
- Delegate or hire out tasks when appropriate.

5. Crises

- Don't allow other people to create a crisis, then expect you to resolve it. Be able to say no and mean it.
- Not all crises need immediate attention. If possible, schedule a time to handle a problem and continue on with your planned tasks.
- Set time aside to anticipate and plan for potential problems and solutions. Keep your schedule flexible.

6. Travel Time

- Be careful to schedule calls for best travel efficiency. Consider traffic such as rush hours.
- Get a car phone. Listen to self-improvement tapes while traveling.

Time Management and the Telephone

Telephones are always a big item when people discuss better time management. Often people have an inability to reduce or stop social chitchat, to terminate their calls, and fear that to do so may offend callers. Here are some suggestions:

- Oversocializing can steal valuable time. Sometimes unnecessary socializing may come from habit, ego, a fear of missing something, a desire to be liked, or even a way to procrastinate. Think carefully about your own telephone habits and recognize your actions for what they are. You can reduce how much time you socialize without offending.
- Tell long-winded callers you have another call coming in, someone just walked in to see you, an appointment arrived, or an emergency is taking place. Do whatever you must to terminate time wasters.
- Don't worry so much that people will become offended. Most people do not offend as easily as we may believe. You do not have to be rude, but you must have the courage to take charge and be firm.
- When practical, group your outgoing calls.
- Plan your calls. Have everything at hand and be organized. Know in advance what you plan to achieve.
- Let voice mail or an answering machine take your calls for certain blocks of time to avoid distractions while you are working on projects.

Sales Call Reluctance

Sales-call reluctance is simply salespeople avoiding what they know they must do—sell. It's a form of procrastination. It means that for some reason, they are uncomfortable with the selling process.

Because they know it is their job to sell, they engage in what is called avoidance behavior. That is to say they find reasons and excuses to delay or avoid the selling process. That way they can justify their behavior. Here are some reasons why people do this:

1. They are not motivated by the project's importance.

2. They con themselves into thinking there will be more time or perhaps it will be easier to do the job another day or time.

3. They are not pressed by anyone to do the task.

4. They have little control over their working environment. They allow a continuous flow of interruptions and disturbances to prevent them from doing meaningful work for any long period of time.

5. Their working environment is cluttered and disorganized. It provides a constant stream of interruptions and distractions, causing interference with their ability to concentrate on the job at hand.

6. They procrastinate so often it becomes a habit.

7. They dread doing the task.

The last one, dreading doing the task, is the main reason for people not making sales calls. It's simply fear of rejection.

A 10-point Plan to Break the Sales Call Reluctance Habit—Now

1. Use a planner or calendar system to keep track of your tasks.

2. Have priorities attached to everything you do; tackle the "A" items first.

3. Start your mornings out with your most difficult tasks, while your energy is fresh.

4. Have a working environment that allows you to focus your concentration.

5. Don't permit interruptions to control your life. Finish one task before you get involved in something else.

6. Learn to say no. Don't allow others to get you involved in situations you really don't have time for.

7. Make it a habit to study the art of selling and the business field you are in on a regular basis. The more you understand, the more you'll feel comfortable doing.

8. Listen to tapes and read books on self-esteem and assertiveness topics regularly.

9. Keep in mind we never get more time. We have to use what time we have to its best advantage.

10. Start *now*!

If you experience fear or its twin, anxiety, you are not alone. Many people are very uncomfortable calling on strangers, especially if they are going to experience rejection repeatedly. In sales, most of the people you call on will have no need for what you sell.

Understand their rejection is not personal to you, but rather they are rejecting the idea of buying what you sell. People who experience this fear or anxiety the most are those with lower self-esteem.

You can work on improving your self-esteem by reading books and listening to audiotapes that discuss self-esteem issues and assertiveness issues. In many areas there are self-help groups that meet to discuss these issues. There are also therapists who can offer help in this area.

I want you to remember, there is no shame in having a self-esteem problem; it's common to some degree in much of the population. The only shame is in not doing something about it.

Starting Your Own Time-management Program

Good time management requires a few simple tools. The most important is an appointment book. Time management is considered so critical with so many businesspeople that there is a wide selection of various time-management products on the market.

Talk to successful executives and they'll swear by their personal time manager. For many years I used a pocket Day-Timer with great results. My brother uses a larger notebook-style planner. He feels it's the only way to go. Your time-manager book is an individual choice and becomes part of you, like family.

Some time-management books are sold by mail order; others are available at office-supply stores. Appendix A lists some of the most popular of these books, along with addresses and phone numbers where you can call or write for a catalog.

I strongly recommend you see what choices are available to you. There is a difference in systems and finding one you feel comfortable with is important to your continuing use of it. Another point to consider is simplicity. The simpler it is to use, the more you'll tend to use it.

To get you started, examples of effective time-management tools are illustrated in this chapter. I'm going to share with you a very effective yet simple way to use these for your small business and sales success.

Step 1—Time Available to Sell

Refer to the illustration, My Prime Selling Hours (Figure 14.1). Because this book is designed to help you sell more, the prime reason for all this activity is to enable you to get out and sell. Therefore, we start with the hours you are going to commit exclusively to selling activity.

There are only three kinds of selling activity we count for this time:

1. *Face-to-face sales calls,* including travel time. This is where you have an appointment to call on a prospect.

2. *Telemarketing for appointments* (or in some situations, actually selling by telephone).

3. *Cold calls.* You simply knock on doors, using strategies from the sections in this book on prospecting.

4. Stop at #3. There are no more activities that count as prime selling hour activities.

Prime selling time is extremely limited even for full-time salespeople, let alone individuals who must also be responsible for a business. For any person who hopes to earn an income from selling, this time is almost sacred.

I don't know what you are selling or to whom, but in general terms, here's a breakdown of prime selling time for a salesperson selling to business firms. Mondays through Fridays, 8:00 A.M. to 11:30 A.M. and 1:30 P.M. to 4:00 P.M. You'll find, as a general rule, many people take lunch between 11:30 A.M. and 1:30 P.M. Trying to sell executives after 4:00 P.M. again can be a problem.

Selling to people individually, in their homes, usually means between the hours of 6:00 P.M. and 9:00 P.M. Monday through Friday.

My Prime Selling Hours

Time I will devote to nothing but face-to-face selling or telemarketing

		Daily total
Monday	A.M. ____ to ____ P.M. ____ to ____	_____
Tuesday	A.M. ____ to ____ P.M. ____ to ____	_____
Wednesday	A.M. ____ to ____ P.M. ____ to ____	_____
Thursday	A.M. ____ to ____ P.M. ____ to ____	_____
Friday	A.M. ____ to ____ P.M. ____ to ____	_____
Saturday	A.M. ____ to ____ P.M. ____ to ____	_____
Sunday	A.M. ____ to ____ P.M. ____ to ____	_____

Weekly total _____

INSTRUCTIONS: To maximize your time for greatest sales efficiency, use this form to determine the times when you must do nothing else but make sales calls. Identify the days and times of day when you can best reach prospects. On the days you don't work, simply enter a zero. Add up the daily hours, and at the bottom add up the total for the week.

Figure 14.1 My prime selling hours.

Often, you can schedule Saturday-morning appointments, say 10:00 A.M. to 1:00 P.M. effectively. Weekdays, many people don't arrive home from work before 5:30 P.M. or 6:00 P.M. Many people use Saturday afternoons to run errands, shop, and so on. Always remember, when selling to couples, *both* need to be available for a sales presentation.

Some products or services lend themselves to different hours. I know a woman who sells cosmetics. She makes sales calls at lunch time to working women. Prime selling hours must be individually determined for what you sell. This allows you to make sales calls at the best time and determine what time to do other, nonselling tasks.

Unless you sell something that really lends itself to this, I'd avoid Sunday sales calls. For the most part it's hard to get an appointment, especially if you need to have more than one person in a meeting. Often it's difficult to get people's attention and commitment on a Sunday. (An exception: I know a man who sells robes to religious groups. Sundays are very busy as well as profitable for him.)

Depending on what other responsibilities you have, I'd suggest starting with 10 to 20 hours per week of selling activities. Under 10 hours per week and you won't really get enough results. If you can schedule more than 20, by all means do so.

Step 2—Schedule Nonselling Work Hours

Everything else you do is scheduled on the sheet, My Nonselling Work Hours (Figure 14.2). This includes sales support activities. For instance, let's say as part of a telemarketing program you're going to mail out 15 or 20 sales letters (or brochures) to a list of suspects. You then plan to wait three or four business days and call these people during your prime selling hours.

Any time you spend looking up addresses at the library, ordering printing, designing, or writing the letters, addressing envelopes, and so on is considered a sales-support activity. That means the time spent is part of your nonselling work hours.

While these are sales activities in a sense, they can't make you a dime. The only thing that will really make you money is making the sales calls. If you don't contact people, either in person or by phone, at least 10 hours or more per week, all the sales-support activities in the world are meaningless.

Step 3—Understand Call Reluctance

Why am I so insistent about this point? Because I know many people will do everything in the world except make the calls. We used to call it "getting ready to get ready." Spending hours developing prospect lists. Sending out direct mail in large quantities hoping people will call you and save you from calling them. Shuffling papers and developing all kinds of systems and things to do.

My Nonselling Work Hours

Preparing reports, returning customer calls, handling customer complaints, performing customer service, developing proposals, and all other nonselling work

Daily
total

Monday	A.M. ____ to ____	P.M. ____ to ____	_____
Tuesday	A.M. ____ to ____	P.M. ____ to ____	_____
Wednesday	A.M. ____ to ____	P.M. ____ to ____	_____
Thursday	A.M. ____ to ____	P.M. ____ to ____	_____
Friday	A.M. ____ to ____	P.M. ____ to ____	_____
Saturday	A.M. ____ to ____	P.M. ____ to ____	_____
Sunday	A.M. ____ to ____	P.M. ____ to ____	_____

Weekly total _____

INSTRUCTIONS: To maximize your time for greatest sales efficiency, use this form to determine the times when you can do the nonsales work of your job. Identify the days and times of day when you can best perform these activities. Make sure they do not conflict with your prime selling hours. On the days you don't work, simply enter a zero. Add up the daily hours, and at the bottom add up the total for the week.

Figure 14.2 My nonselling work hours.

People who delay making calls are usually the same people who consistently take sales courses and are always buying books, looking for something new. What they secretly hope to find does not exist—a way to sell without making the calls. "You gotta make calls if you wanna get results!" I can still hear an old sales manager saying that to our staff. It is as true today as it was then.

Step 4—"Take the Bull by the Horns"

In other sections of this book I've suggested ideas to help you overcome this feeling of not wanting to make sales calls. There's one more idea I'll share with you now.

Simply force yourself to do what you fear. My mother used to say, "Just take the bull by the horns and go ahead." (My mom was raised on a farm in Missouri.) Ever hear the phrase, "Just do it!" ? That's what it means. Recognize you feel uncomfortable, understand it's necessary for your business survival, and just do it!

Finally, remember this little gem: What's the worst that can happen? If you make a sales call and they don't want to buy from you, so what? Do you really expect everybody, every time will buy? Of course not. You know from reading this book most people will reject your offer.

Notice I said, "reject your offer." That's not the same as rejecting you. It simply means they have no need for what you sell at this time. Accept it, live with it. It's no big deal, to them or to you. Go on to your next call.

I promise you this, the law of averages alone will protect you if you persevere, if you don't let a little rejection stand in your way. That's because as you make those calls, mixed in with the people who say no are people who are looking for someone like you—people with problems your product or service can solve. People who need you.

Step 5—Your Weekly Success Plan

To be effective on a consistent basis, you need a work plan. My Weekly Success Plan (Figure 14.3) is a simple yet effective planning sheet. Take a legal pad and hand copy the key parts. It's important that this be filled out as completely as possible at the very beginning of the week. I'm not talking about doing this Monday morning. That's prime time, either for selling or for getting things accomplished in your business. I mean fill this out on a Sunday evening so when you arrive at work on Monday morning your mind is already

---

*My Weekly Success Plan - Week of*_____

Goals and objectives I plan to accomplish by this week's end

Daily activities needed to accomplish weekly goals	Day	Priority	Time Required

Figure 14.3 My weekly success plan.

focused on what needs to be done. One secret of success is getting a good start to your work week.

There are two resources to consult when filling this sheet out. The first is your 90-Day Goal Form, discussed in the previous chapter. The second is the two selling and nonselling hours work sheets we've discussed in this chapter. From these, you can decide not only what you want to get done, but when you'll do it.

Step 6—Your Daily Success Plan

One critical form I have left out is your daily work plan and appointment form. I did that for a reason. Earlier I told you that Appendix A lists several resources for time-management tools. In addition, office-supply stores sell other products. (There are so many it's impossible to list everything.)

The daily appointment form is the most important of your work sheets and I want you to decide, without any influence from me, what best fits your needs. Buying the most expensive, the fanciest, the name brand, the impressive leather case, and so on has absolutely nothing to do with your success. I have seen some of the most successful salespeople you'd ever meet use little ragged books they purchased at a discount store. Don't get caught up in fancy.

Look at the time-management tools and decide if they are practical for you. Can you see yourself using them, day in and day out? Some of them are systems and have forms for goals and longer-term commitments that will replace the forms I've illustrated in this book. As you shop, you'll see what makes sense and when you see it, "Just do it!"

Finally, I use a set of time-management forms in my seminars, some of which are illustrated in this book. If you'd like to find out about them, refer to Appendix E.

15

Tools and Techniques to Increase Productivity

If you are running a small business by yourself or if you are a part of a small business organization you may realize how unimportant job titles are. One moment you are the salesperson, the next the order-filling clerk, and a little later, the delivery person. Rules for success in the small business are somewhat different from those in large corporate America.

The keyword for your continued success here is diversity—being able to do multiple jobs, successfully, often at the same time. Owning the proper tools requires an investment you must really be willing and financially able to make. When you own the proper tools, your ability to function in several roles becomes possible.

BEFORE YOU INVEST A PENNY

What you'll need for even a very small, one-person business is a computer, laser printer, fax machine, and voice-mail machine. Before you invest a penny, you must know what's available, what you can buy for the amount of money you can afford, and, most importantly, you should understand computers enough to operate one and comparison shop intelligently.

WHAT YOU NEED

Technology is changing at a very rapid rate. What is current as I write this will not necessarily be the latest or the best buy by the time you read it. For that reason I'm not going to be too specific. I'm a big believer in taking advantage of the best technology available at the time.

One small warning: When you mention buying a computer, some people start complaining about how the technology is changing so fast and how you'd better wait until things settle down so you don't pay too much and on and on. Please, don't listen to them. This is unrealistic thinking. The only people you'll hear talking like that are either totally uneducated in computers, have a very limited knowledge of computers, or are too cheap to buy one and want to justify their tight-fisted behavior.

You are buying this equipment for a business venture and if you're totally honest with yourself, for a little personal pleasure also. Once you have studied the market and understand what to buy, do so. There is not now, nor will there ever be, a right time when you can buy a computer and it won't be obsolete in a few years. Who cares? The point of a computer is to get you into the business world in a competitive way. By the time it has become obsolete, it will have paid you back many times whatever you invested in it.

The world is advancing every year at a faster and faster pace. I don't know about you, but I'm in awe of it. I'm old enough to remember when all the electronics advances we see today were considered science fiction. I love going into computer stores just to see what's new.

As I write this, computers using the Windows environment are far and away the most common technology, although a few others are now trying to compete. What it boils down to is that by buying the most common, you can find a bigger selection of software and obtain help more easily.

Make sure the computer will have enough hard-drive storage space to hold all the software you plan to install now plus some room for future expansion. As I write this, my best guess is at least a hard drive with 1 gigabyte storage (that's 1,000 megabytes). For some people who now own computers, that may sound like overkill. It isn't. As computer software evolves, it becomes more useful and productive. However, each new version with its improvements takes up more of your hard-drive storage.

You'll also want to buy a computer with a large enough RAM memory to operate your software comfortably. As I write this 8 megabytes is the least you should buy. As Windows '95 and its successors become common, programs will come into popular use that require 16 megabytes.

The computer you buy should also have an internal fax and telephone modem. Some come with built-in telephone voice-mail answering systems.

A CD-ROM drive should have at least 6X or better access speed.

A scanner is an option to consider seriously. It allows you to scan printed designs such as company logos and artwork into a file in your computer so you can reproduce them. It can also scan pages of text and with a computer program (most come with the software to do this), you can turn the scanned page into text in your computer's word processing program. If you are going to do a lot of desktop publishing, scanners are a very useful tool and a wise investment.

A Computer

To start with, you need a computer. I don't care if you are a young person who's used them in school or an old codger who's scared of learning something new. People in business today without a computer, even one person working from his or her home, handicap their opportunity for success. Computers today are user friendly and not that hard to learn to use, even for the novice.

Buying a computer first and understanding it after you've paid for it is a big, big mistake. There simply is no way to make an intelligent purchase of something you don't understand. If you are depending on other people to help you make that decision you will then have to live with what they think is important, not you. If you are not computer literate, the first place to go is a computer-training source. You can find them offered in several places:

1. Look in the yellow pages. There are computer-training organizations that do nothing but that.

2. Call the colleges and universities in your area. Most have a continuing adult-education department where you can take evening classes.

3. Call the high schools. Some of those also have evening classes for adults.

4. Stores that sell computers often have training programs and trainers available. Find out if you save any money on the training if you purchase a computer from them.

5. Many people buy computers to make money at home. Ask around and watch bulletin boards for advertisements. One of those people might be willing to help you to learn about computers.

Subscribe to a few computer magazines and devote some time on a regular basis to reading them. If you are new to computers there a few publications that advertise they are for novice users.

A Printer

When you operate a small business you want to project success and competency. Many people many never see where you work, but they will see materials, such as price lists, price quotations, letters, brochures, and so on, that represent you. Many will judge you based on what they see. For that reason, a good computer printer is essential.

Currently, there are several kinds of computer printers. The lowest quality is dot-matrix. While suitable for some situations, I don't recommend them for any business. The output from them, even the very best models, is crude compared with other choices. Using a dot-matrix printer to print important documents makes you look small, crude, and flimsy.

Inkjet printers are next in quality (and price). If money is a big issue, then they are an okay choice. Most of them print very slowly, which can be a problem if you produce a lot of output.

Laser printers are really the best way to go. While they cost a little more, they can save you money in several other ways. Consider the savings you may incur with a laser printer before you make any decisions. The lower-end models also print slowly, but as you step up in price, the speed picks up. One reason I like the laser is that, with some inexpensive software, you can create and print your own business cards and stationery. With a laser you also can design and print your own flyers, brochures, labels, postcards, and direct-mail pieces. Many people use laser printers to produce newsletters. There are numerous companies that preprint interesting borders and other designs on sheets of paper, leaving the center blank. (I've listed several in Appendix C that send out very nice catalogs showing you the variety of materials available.) You can use your laser printer to print your sales messages in the open areas. If you have a good desktop publishing program you can do the same thing with blank sheets. When finished, these folders, labels, newsletters, postcards, and brochures have a very professional appearance.

A laser printer allows a small company with limited resources to present a very professional look. Since you print these materials yourself, you can make as many or as few as needed. If you have a company logo you can have it scanned into a computer file and reproduce it on all your printed materials. Again, this presents a more professional image for the small company.

If you do presentations such as speeches, workshops, training sessions, or seminars a laser printer can be used to print custom overhead presentation transparencies you design in your computer.

Do you need color? It makes a more interesting print, but color machines cost much more and since they are more complicated machines, have higher upkeep costs for repairs and supplies. Unless color has a valuable use in your business, I'd stick to a standard printer.

Computer Software

Many computers come with free installed programs. Some may be useful but I'd leave some money in the budget for buying additional software. A word of warning: To save a few bucks, some computer companies install software but don't give you a set of the original disks. Also, sometimes the manuals they give are flimsy, cut-down versions of the original.

I don't care how dependable the computer maker claims your hard drive is, the fact remains that it can crash and leave you with no software. What can happen even more frequently is that you may erase or badly damage a program through your own error. I've been using computers almost every day for over 10 years. Just a few months ago, when trying to correct a problem, I pushed the wrong key. To make a long, sad story short I damaged my program and had no choice but to reinstall it from my original computer disks. If I didn't have those disks I would have had run to a computer store and try to buy that program's software. If it wasn't easily available I'd have had to take time to shop for something else, come back to the office, install it, and then take time to learn the new program. When you run any size business, you work with deadlines. Don't trust your business records to exist just in the machine. Keep back-up programs and data of critical records.

Business Software You May Consider

Spreadsheet

Commonly used for accounting and financial analysis. The earlier versions were difficult for nonfinancial people to understand. The newer programs are much more user friendly.

Accounting

For a small business a simple program is usually best. I've used the one from Intuit called "Quickbooks." They also publish the program "Quicken," which is far and away the best (and easiest) home checkbook and financial software program I've ever seen.

Database

A database program is used to gather, sort, collate, and edit information. You can also apply mathematical formulas, print mailing lists or labels, as well as perform other functions. My personal experience is that database programs are invaluable for mailing and prospect lists. Unless you are very experienced with these programs, buy the simplest and most user-friendly one available.

Word Processing

The first programs allowed you to use your computer as a typewriter with all the advantages of a computer. More recent versions are starting to cross over and perform desktop publishing tasks as well. A good program should include a built-in spelling checker and thesaurus. I wrote this book on a word processing program from Lotus Development Corporation.

Desktop Publishing

A valuable tool, especially for small businesspeople who can't afford professionals to do their layout and design work for flyers and so on. If you have little experience and your initial needs are not very complicated, get a simple program, not the top of the line. While the bigger programs do really great things, they take a lot of time and effort to learn.

Contact Management

Contact-management software programs are like an electronic address book, but because it's in a computer you can do much more. For instance, you can record appointments in the software. You can look someone up and have the computer, through your modem, dial the person. Some programs will also do word processing and fax messages. There are several programs available and you need to do a little shopping before making a final decision. *One warning*: Some people use these programs for large-scale telemarketing. It's rather awkward to work a telemarketing operation from any of the ones I've seen. They really are not designed for that purpose. Purchase a program specifically designed for telemarketing.

How to Select the Right Software for Your Needs

There's nothing worse than going through the steps to buy, install, and learn to use a new computer program, and then when you start to use it, find it is not right for what you are doing. That, in a nutshell, is what sometimes happens when you decide by just reading the boxes in the computer store or by asking the salespeople.

There are several excellent computer magazines published in this country. It's a good idea to subscribe to at least one or you can read these free at the library. They all review various computer software programs. Reading these reviews, written by people who have actually used these programs, can be a real eye-opener. They also let you know about programs not commonly available in the retail computer stores that may be a big help to you.

Fax Machines

In today's business world a fax machine is standard. Many new computers come equipped with a built-in fax and telephone modem. A stand-alone fax can double as an office copier if you make only a few copies a month.

I've communicated with other business firms by typing letters on a letterhead design in my computer, then sending the file by fax machine to the recipients' computers. They may read it, then delete it. In essence, what I have done is send a letter with no paper, no postage, and no post office and it gets there in seconds, not days! If you communicate to out-of-town firms that have equipment to receive fax transmissions, you can program your fax to transmit in the middle of the night or on weekends, when the rates are dirt cheap—often much cheaper than the cost of postage.

Copy Machines

While a stand-alone fax machine can double as a copy machine for a few copies, it is not practical for more intense usage. The same is true for laser printers. They are not practical for large runs. Making an original on your laser and then using a copy machine for the larger quantities is usually the best solution.

There are several low-end copy machines suitable for small business. The best way to buy one is to visit stores where they are on actual display. Have a knowledgeable person explain the features of the various models. Even if you are set on a low-end unit, let the salesperson explain the better models to you and the price difference. In a small business or home office you'll have the machine a very long time before you wear it out. Sometimes the additional features are worth the few dollars extra rather than struggling to use a low-end machine and putting extra hours of labor into a minor task.

Remember, your time has value. In a small business where one person or just a few people do everything, it's often cheaper to let a better machine do the work while you focus your efforts on important issues, such as sales.

Telephones

A separate line dedicated to your business is a good idea. Be very careful how it is answered. A professional method would be a voice-mail system when you are not there. You can get inexpensive systems that can be installed into your computer. In fact, some machines come equipped with them.

In my area of the country the telephone company provides voice mail for a few dollars a month. I have it on a single telephone line. If I'm talking on the phone, instead of a busy signal the caller gets my voice mail. The next time I pick up my telephone to make a call, the dial tone makes a rapid signaling noise to let me know I have a voice-mail message.

Telephone answering machines are not an option anymore for businesses. Voice mail is so inexpensive, few business firms use telephone answering machines. If you do, you really look unprofessional.

If you work from home, allowing children to answer a business line is very unprofessional.

A second line, dedicated to your fax machine, is also a good idea if you have a heavy volume of calls. If you do business outside your immediate area code, check out the possibility of an 800 phone line. The rates are very reasonable.

16

"If You Were My Best Friend"

STARTING FROM SCRATCH

If you were my best friend and told me you were seriously considering starting your own business, this chapter and the next chapter are what I'd share with you.

Successful selling in your own business is nothing like selling as an employee in someone else's. When you sell for someone else, you only need concern yourself with making the sale. When you sell in your own business, making the sale is sometimes the easy part. You have also the responsibility to satisfy the customer, make a profit and, oh yes, turn out the lights when you go home.

I've been there. I've run a small business and done the selling. Actually I've owned or been a principal in several successful businesses. The mistakes I made in those early years could fill another book. In those tough early days I had times when I wasn't sure I could make a go of it all—times when I wasn't sure how I could make the next payroll. However, I survived. I actually made a good living after I got the hang of things. I just wish someone would have told me then what I'm about to tell you.

This chapter is dedicated to the men and women reading this book who own their own business and are responsible not only for the sales, but for the ultimate success or failure of the business. The chapter will cover issues you must deal with as you develop a selling plan. As the owner of a business you'll find that selling is a whole lot more than writing an order. You will also find that once you write that order, you assume a lot of responsibilities. I want to share with you the sum total of my own hard-learned lessons.

It's about issues directly connected to the selling process. As a small businessperson what you do and how you do it has some pretty big consequences. The success or failure of your business could hinge on what you do and how you do it to sell your products or services. It is something I've personally faced several times in my life. So, please read this chapter carefully. It will give you the vital information necessary to formulate an effective selling plan, a plan to make your business prosper for a long time to come.

BEATING THE AVERAGES

The failure rate of new businesses is dismal, especially smaller ones. Most fail totally. But even worse is the living hell some people endure in small businesses that make just enough not to die, yet not enough to pay their owner a decent living. I know of small business-owners who have been around for 20 years or more and have done nothing but live day to day, always just one step ahead of bill collectors and tax people for the whole 20 years. That's no way to live.

A business needs to earn enough money to pay its debt in a timely fashion. It also needs to pay its owner a living wage to support the owner's own needs and expectations. If it doesn't do that, it's a loser. It's no secret why the majority of these businesses either fail or struggle forever in mediocrity. The most frequent answer is simply a lack of sales. The businesses that fail, in most cases, are the ones that don't have enough customers willing to pay a fair price for the services or goods the business produces.

But take heart. There's no reason to fail. There's no reason to struggle in mediocrity. The unfortunate people who do fail or struggle with minimal success very frequently do so because they know so little about the selling process.

Selling skills are a major key to the success of any business. Since many people fear selling (we'll discuss how to deal with that in detail below), they try to avoid facing it. They may try to hire someone to do the selling job for them, which, in the beginning, is a mistake.

LEARNING BY SELLING

When you are selling your product or services personally, you have direct contact with potential customers. You have the advantage of the immediate feedback. If your services or product(s) have weaknesses, this is where you find out. I know, some people hate to hear bad news. But if there's bad news to hear, it's vital to your business success for you to hear it first. It's also your job to do every reasonable thing you can to fix the problem.

By making the direct-sales contact with clients you'll also be gaining invaluable information about your business potential and what it takes to build a successful business in the long haul. When you eventually hire others to handle the selling function, your own experience will aid you immensely in developing your company policies and in directing employees' attitudes toward customers.

I have a sign in my office that says: "If we don't take care of our customers, someone else will." In the competitive world of business, it's a truth you must never forget. You will learn things about your business when you sell that you really can't learn elsewhere. You will have personal contact with customers and potential customers. You'll soon learn what it takes to make a sale, what it takes to make a profit, what kinds of customers you'll really want, and what customers are not very desirable. In short, you'll learn the business from the bottom up, which is the very best way to start out.

Even if you can afford to hire a salesperson early on in your business, forget it. *You* be the salesperson. Hire people if you must to do office work or production work or whatever else you do. *You* take the sales responsibility in the beginning. I promise you, it's money in the bank.

BAD STARTS: WHERE MOST BUSINESS FAILURES ARE CREATED

Bad starts are where most business troubles begin. A bad start guarantees frustration and hardship. Let's discuss the major areas where small businesses fail. These are directly related to the selling process so please don't skip this section.

You can't build a house without first laying a foundation. If you just start to put up walls and a roof the whole thing will collapse under its own weight after a short time. Sure, it may look great for a little while, but it can't last. It's the same with any business. If you don't have means of delivering your products or services, if you don't have a sales contract, if you don't have a way to deal with customers uniformly, every sale you make can lead to grief.

Simply put, when you go out and make a sale to a new customer for your product or service, you are entering into a contract with all the liabilities and responsibilities that go with it. Even if you work from your home and do business on a handshake, the law gives your customers certain legal rights.

As a sales consultant I often see small businesspeople sell themselves into serious problems. They do business without considering the ramifications of their actions. They also make a common erroneous assumption that all their customers will be completely honest and treat them fairly.

My own experience is that most customers are basically nice, honest people. However, even the finest of people still have their own self-interests at heart (just as you should) and if they feel things are not as promised (in their opinion), they will come after you with a vengeance.

It does not matter if you have a business that has been around for quite some time or are just starting up. If you plan on reaching a profitable goal, you must start with a strong foundation. What if your business is already established and as you read these basics you realize you have not addressed them? Don't worry, you can still go back. It's not as easy as establishing them right from the beginning, but you can and should still address them.

Here are five major reasons new business ventures fail. The sad thing is that with a little time and patience, they can be corrected. Read carefully.

1. No Business Plan

This tops the list. People get an idea, talk to a few other people who like the idea, and suddenly fall in love with the idea. They can't wait to run out and start the new business. In their eagerness to make a million, they don't sit down and write out a business plan. They go out and learn the whole thing by trial and error. Somewhere along the line they either run out of money or find out their idea wasn't so good after all. They become another business failure. The worst part is that I've seen people use every borrowed and begged dollar they could get, only to lose every penny this way.

A business plan is no more than a written outline of how you plan to run your business. It's a way of looking into the future of your business idea on paper, before you've invested big money. It's one way to prove to yourself that your idea has merit. If you find your plan showing a lot of negative situations, then allow reality to set in and consider if this is really the right move.

One reason people don't use a business plan is that they can be rather complex. I've read some business-plan books that become very difficult to follow. In our modern electronic age, however, there are some really great solutions for the average person who may have little or no business experience. The answer is computers.

Frankly I don't see anyone going into business today without a computer. I know that sounds scary to some, but the new computers today are very easy to learn. High schools, colleges, trade schools, and large computer retailers are excellent sources of evening classes for the novice. Considering the other costs of starting up any business, even from a home, a computer should be part of your initial plans.

There are several manufacturers of business-plan software, many designed for the inexperienced user. I've seen programs that take very little learning. They ask you a series of questions which, when answered, will work up a business plan. I don't want you to think this is a one-evening project, it isn't. The questions asked may send you out to do some research, but this is necessary in order to know yourself and your potential business.

If you really get stuck on a business plan, here are a few good ways to get help:

1. Get help from a CPA or attorney who has experience writing these. Be careful that they have this experience, since many don't.

2. Find the nearest university or business college. Ask the people who teach business if they would like to do your business plan as a class project. Many colleges like to have their students work in the real world on projects such as this. Costwise, this is very inexpensive and, if the instructor is overseeing and supervising the effort, you should have a decent plan with no big money involved.

   There are two downsides to this way. First, students can get off in the wrong direction because they are new to this. Second, this is usually a long-term project that can take several months to complete.

3. Most business colleges have professors who moonlight and will take on such a project for a fee.

4. Advertise! One of the best ways I know to hire *any* professional help on a part-time or temporary basis is to place a classified ad in a well-read Sunday paper. There are thousands of highly paid professionals in fields such as writing, public relations, advertising, layout and design, accounting, legal, and much more.

   I'm speaking about highly paid professionals who now work and who you could probably not afford to pay their regular salary. Many will moonlight evenings and weekends at very reasonable rates to augment their salary. Here's an example ad (slightly disguised) I ran for a client recently:

   > ADVERTISING WRITER. Part/spare time to assist small business develop brochures. Hourly. Resume to: Box 123, Newspaper, 4567 Main St., Yourtown, ST.

   I'll explain in more detail how to use this strategy in the next chapter under strategy 13.

If you already own a small business and don't have a business plan you can do this also. There's no law that says business plans are only written for start-ups. You may learn some surprising (and profitable) things about your existing business by doing this exercise.

2. Not Understanding Your Customers

A lot of people in start-up businesses have no idea why people buy from them. They fall in love with their business and can't see why everyone else doesn't feel the same way.

People buy for many reasons. For instance, they may not even like you, but if your product or service is the only convenient resource, they'll still come. However, let a new competitor, perhaps more likable, show up, you're out! Or say they buy because you're a few cents cheaper than anyone else; the minute a competitor cuts prices, you're history!

You must know how your customer perceives you. When times are tough and competitors start taking away your business, your knowledge will help you devise new marketing strategies. The business firm that understands its customers' wants and needs is very hard to beat.

Here's an example. I'm using retail business firms in this example, but it applies to all businesses. Where I live, several major food chains have built "super stores." These are very large facilities with multiple services. In addition to buying the week's groceries from a very large selection of products, you can eat lunch, do your banking, buy flowers, buy fresh-baked goods, and so on. One huge retailer started the trend when they moved in from out of town, built two new super stores, and promised to blanket our town with several new ones within two years. They spoke of taking over the food business in my community. I'm sure they scared the daylights out of the existing food retailers. When they first opened, they were mobbed. The older, smaller stores in town were a lot less crowded.

Over time, two things happened. Some smaller stores went out of business. They didn't have the money to compete. Sad, yes, but the truth is they were in over their heads. They did the right thing. It's better to know when to fold your tent, take your resources, and start over in a less-demanding market or perhaps a different business. The worst thing to do is to stick it out bravely until the bitter end and spend your last dime trying to keep a dead business alive. You'll still go out, but then you won't have the resources to start over. A few words from one of country singer Kenny Rogers' songs—"...you've got to know when to hold them, know when to fold them..."—holds great truth in more than a card game.

The second thing I saw happen was that some of the older, established stores somehow found the money to enlarge and modernize their facilities. Pretty soon, they also were "super stores." The last I heard about the huge out-of-town retailer was that they have shelved plans to expand for the present. I visited one of their stores recently. They still do business, but the original crowds of customers have long since gone. They've closed down some of the inside booths offering a variety of services and the facilities show signs of wear and lack of attention. In short, the place looks beat. Have they captured a share of the food business in my community? Yes. Have they taken over the market? Hardly.

The reason most of the local food merchants prevailed was that they had a clear vision of why customers came to them. In this case it was shopping convenience. Knowing that, they took steps to keep pace with a trend and thus kept most of their customers. The people who didn't really know or could not keep the pace are gone.

3. Doing Everything Yourself

This may seem like a contradiction. I just told you to go out and be your own salesperson. Now I'm telling you to hire people. It isn't. There's a time and place in every business for both.

In the beginning stages, it is imperative you learn the business of selling your products or services. If you can't do it, how can you expect others to? If you already have an established business and sales stink, then again, you are the only person who should go out to correct it. You've got to understand your customers at that level before you can really plan growth.

Sometimes in my consulting business I'll suggest to a businessperson that he or she needs to hire help. The most common response is, "I can't afford it." It's the worst possible answer you can give. Let me show you why.

Remember at the start of this chapter I discussed business firms that have gone out of business and others that stay in business for years, barely surviving, the owner living hand to mouth for years? That's the kind of response these people give. It's one of the big reasons they can never grow, expand, and, of course, become more profitable. Don't be one of them.

When a business doesn't have money to grow with, it's dying. Forget all the face-saving excuses why, it's still dying. In order to succeed in business, you must grow; otherwise you shrink.

If you don't have the money to invest into the business to hire help, keep equipment updated, maintain property, and so on, you are not making enough profits. Few new businesspeople understand how much profit is necessary for a business to succeed. Newcomers to business sometimes report they feel a secret shame if they charge too much, perhaps feeling people will look down on them as being greedy.

This is another reason a business plan is vital to your success. It identifies the obvious costs of business such as lights, heat, telephone, and so on. A good plan will also identify the more hidden but very necessary costs of hiring help at certain stages, expanding and maintaining any necessary facilities and equipment, and all of the other hidden business costs you're going to have to face. Most importantly, it will allow you to plug in a living wage for yourself.

A lot of the newcomers often confuse company income with personal income. If you start a new business, you are entitled to take out a living wage. In the beginning, many people work for free to get started. That's okay to a point, depending on your finances. At some time in your business plan, you must decide a specific time when the business will pay you a living wage. Usually this is the critical point for a new business. When this time arrives, many can't pay the owner a living wage, so he or she "steals" a few dollars from money destined for taxes or creditors and hopes for the best.

This is really a time when you must decide if you close the business or if you can bring it up to speed. Again, with a business plan you can compare your projections to what is really happening. Sometimes this will be the information you need to get the business on track and making money. Other times, it will help you to decide to close. Without this kind of knowledge, you can founder for years.

4. Not Enough Cash

A business plan should also show you how much cash is needed to run your business (called a cash-flow projection). If you collect cash in advance, that's one thing, but if you must provide service and/or products and then wait for payment, it's another. You need to decide on who gets credit, and if they do, for how long.

Keep cash flowing when you make sales by getting advance payments and limiting credit. Just because all your competitors give credit does not mean you have to (and don't believe they are as liberal as prospects claim they are).

5. Not Knowing, or Ignoring the Numbers

Keep track with good record keeping. Everybody agrees, yet so many businesses keep such miserable records that nobody, including them, knows what's going on.

Successful businesses pay out hard-earned money for accounting services because they know their continued success depends on good record keeping.

Keeping good accounting records used to be a nightmare for me. I did it because I knew my future depended upon it, but I hated every minute of it. I was forever bewildered, always calling my accountant or lawyer on the phone to get records straight. When it came time to bill my monthly customers, I often turned into a raving fool. Doing the process by hand was complicated and often confusing. I always feared making a mistake that could cost my business much-needed revenue.

Then a great and wonderful thing happened to me. I purchased my first computer. It was crude by today's standards, but it was really my savior. For the first time in years I was confident my checkbook really balanced, confident I had not missed billing clients for all services, confident of the P&L statements and balance sheets because I had created them, showing me the critical information I needed daily.

In today's world there are computers much easier to use. There are computerized accounting programs that are designed for small businesses and for users new to them. There are training courses, as

I outlined earlier, to learn computer skills. Your library has books written for nonaccountants to understand basic accounting. You don't require the skills of a CPA or an attorney in business accounting, just some very basic ones to understand balance sheets and P&L statements.

Once you acquire these skills, you'll be completely self-sufficient in your business. Since nobody will care more about your business than you, you will always be the best judge of what's best for your business. You need to be well informed and have the proper tools. While I always recommend my clients hire the best accountants and the best attorneys they can find, I also recommend they do most of the legwork themselves and then use the professional to review and double-check their efforts.

A LEGAL SALES AGREEMENT: DON'T LEAVE THE OFFICE WITHOUT IT

If you are going to sell products or services to anyone, then whenever that event occurs, you need to write it down. For instance, my friend Jim sells paving services. His company is small and he is both manager and salesperson. He does jobs such as driveways for homeowners and parking lots for business firms in his area.

In Jim's business, whenever he has made a sale he writes down everything promised the customer on an order form. This includes the customer's address as well as a space for a different address should he be contracting work at a different location, thickness of paving materials, kind of paving materials, specific areas to be covered, date work shall start, price of work, and so on.

In addition, Jim's sales agreement contains basic information about what he will and won't agree to. For instance, to keep his business insurance low, he has a clause that in the event of an insurance claim, the customer must first contact his insurance carrier. His agreement specifically explains under what circumstances he will guarantee the work performed and under what circumstances he will not. It also allows Jim not to do the work as scheduled in the event of an act of God such as snowstorm, tornado, and so on.

Perhaps the most important is the area for payment terms. It specifically shows the total job price, down payment at time of order (if collected, and you should if possible), the balance due, and when the balance will be paid. In Jim's case, that's upon completion of the job. It's agreed the customer will pay the job foreman in full any balance due.

Why am I suggesting a down payment at the time of sale? Why collect the balance at time of delivery of the products or services? Because in any-size business, the biggest concern is cash flow. You can have millions of dollars in property, equipment, and other assets, but if you don't have enough money in the bank to pay your employees at the end of the week, you're out of business.

I learned this lesson the hard way. I was originally one of those owners/salespeople who felt pretty good when I'd say to a new customer, "Don't worry about payment, you can just drop me a check in the mail." As a salesperson, you are on the front line, making decisions and cutting deals that can have big effects on your company. In a great many instances you can ask for a down payment and request payment be completed at time of delivery. Many small business firms go bankrupt each year because the owner was cavalier about extending credit to anyone with a business name. Later on, when these firms, which also have cash-flow problems, purposely drag payment, especially to small vendors, it's too late.

SUING DEBTORS: A LAST RESORT

Sue them, you say? Sure, go ahead, that'll teach 'em! Over the years I've worked with many collection agencies and attorneys. A good collection attorney is hard to find. When you do find one, here's how it usually breaks down. The attorney will work for a fee of 30 percent to 50 percent of actual moneys collected. In the real world, he or she will rarely collect the full amount. Usually, to avoid going to court (which really drags out the process), the attorney will offer the deadbeat some sort of settlement for a prompt payment, usually fifty cents on the dollar is considered acceptable.

If you want the satisfaction in court, let me show you how quickly your satisfaction will shrink. An account you can't collect after four months for $1,000 is given to an attorney. Three or four months later the attorney settles for $500 to avoid a court fight, the attorney keeping 50 percent of the $500. You get the grand total of $250 eight months late. If you *do* go to court, depending on where you live, it can take six to 12 months' additional time. You will have to appear in court, so there goes a day of your time.

A favorite trick among deadbeats is to wait until everybody has made a specific trip to court, then have some excuse for the judge to continue the matter. That's another totally wasted day of your time. They feel if they stall long enough you'll get tired and not show up for one of the trial dates. That's the day *they* will go to court and you're not there, so guess what? The judge rules in their favor! Although this does not always happen—some judges won't allow cases to be continued more than once—in some situations I have seen it happen repeatedly.

If the judge awards the full amount in your favor you still have to enforce collection, which in some cases is next to impossible. Taking people to court is okay in certain cases. However, I'd strongly advise doing so as a last resort and only when the amount of money involved is worth the struggle.

SALES CONTRACT EXAMPLES

As I said before, if you sell anything to anybody without committing to writing all the terms you and the customer have agreed upon, you invite disaster. A legal sales agreement is the very first thing any business, no matter how small, must have.

You'll need the services of an attorney to review the legal consequences of your document. Your best bet would be an attorney who has worked for other clients in your industry and who may have a working knowledge of your industry's business liabilities. At the least you want an attorney who specializes in contract law.

What constitutes a legal agreement in your business is going to be different in every state. It's going to be different in various kinds of businesses. One thing you must know is that when you do business with someone, you have created a contract. If it's not written then it's what is called implied and you can be held accountable for your actions in a court of law.

A simplified example might be this: I call a lawn service to spray my lawn for insect control. I sign nothing and the company has no agreement or warranty printed. Some person just comes out and sprays my lawn because of my call on the phone. The whole transaction is verbal. While he is working, my dog wanders on the lawn and he gets sick from the chemicals. I pay the driver and he leaves before I discover the damage.

I sue him in court, claiming negligence on his part and demanding he pay me not only for my dog's vet bills, but also damages. He defends himself, saying he told me to keep pets and children away from the lawn during and for six hours after the treatment. I deny that he said anything. Chances are excellent the court will rule in my favor and the lawn service will pay damages. Had that been a child, with serious after-effects, the damages could have bankrupted the lawn contractor.

However, what if the lawn contractor had asked me to sign an order form that contained legal warnings about the lawn treatment? What if it also had a space on it for me to further initial that I was acknowledging my responsibility in keeping the lawn free and clear of any children and pets under my control? What if the lawn contractor further put a couple of small signs in my grass warning people to stay off for 24 hours? Remember, I am not an attorney nor am I offering this as legal advice. In fact, this may not be an acceptable legal solution and is only an example, but I think it clearly shows the point I'm making. That is, get good legal assistance, have a written agreement between you and your customers, and don't do business on a handshake, ever.

A major reason to have a written agreement, besides the threat of a lawsuit, is that of human nature. People who become your customers often have much higher expectations of what your product or service is or will do for them. If you have never done business with people before in a business setting, you're in for a bit of a surprise.

By spelling out exactly what you can (and can't) do for them, you'll eliminate the number of complaints and dissatisfied customers by a big margin. No matter how great you may be, there will be unhappy campers from time to time.

INSURANCE

Finally, let's mention the one big item I left out of these examples, insurance. Again, your business plan needs to include the costs of adequate insurance for your business. Many kinds of insurance are available. I'm not an expert in insurance, yet I know enough from my own experience in business to strongly recommend you carry adequate insurance from the first day of business. When you buy a liability insurance to protect you, the insurance company may make some very helpful, specific suggestions about clauses in your written agreement.

How to buy the right insurance? How not to overbuy insurance? In the end, you're the final judge, but I would suggest this course of action: First, speak to your attorney about your business venture and ask his or her opinion regarding insurance. Second, speak to a CPA and get a second opinion. Third, speak to two or three insurance agents who specialize in your kind of insurance needs. The best way to locate any professional services, such as attorneys, accountants, insurance agents, business consultants, and so on, is to get references from businesspeople you respect.

Don't have an attorney or CPA? This is the time to find one. Insurance and written sales contracts are just the tip of the iceberg. You will also face serious tax questions plus whether to incorporate and if so, how. You don't need the risks and grief. If you feel you can't afford the advice of these kinds of professionals, you really don't belong in business, at least until you have money to get this help. The hazards you face can be very serious.

GETTING UNCLE SAM'S HELP

First, in the planning stages of developing a sales program for your business, you need to consider if the U.S. government might be a prospect for the products or services you can provide. Second, many times while running a small business, questions will come up that you just don't readily find answers for. If you have a small business, the U.S. government provides some business counseling free of charge.

The U.S. government has specifically set aside contracts and portions of contracts for small business, minorities, and women-owned businesses. A great many people don't realize the vast amounts of varied products and services the U.S. government buys every day, all around the world.

While I firmly believe it would be a big mistake to think you should start a business up just to sell the government, it is also a mistake not to explore the opportunities available to you as a small businessperson. Just remember that selling to the government takes a lot of time, patience, and energy. It will be a long time between the time you place your first bid and the time you receive a check for services rendered. As a rule of thumb I would devote no more than 10 percent or 15 percent of my available prospecting time to this. Here are some specifics:

Small Business Administration (SBA). Your first step should be to contact the closest office of the SBA. They will provide you with information about the services they provide and available programs.

Service Corps of Retired Executives (SCORE). SCORE is a division of the SBA. It is comprised of retired executives who donate their time to providing business consulting free of charge to small businesses on request. For instance, if you'd like some advice on finding new markets or hiring sales help, you can ask if they have retired sales or marketing executives available to consult with.

Small Business Development Centers (SDBC) (federal government). You can get a list of SBDCs in your area through SBA. Among other things, they provide low-cost training programs on various aspects of business, including sales and marketing. In my state they also have state-run SBDCs, different from those run by the federal government.

Finding various U.S. and state government offices can be a challenge in itself. Here are a few effective ways to locate those you may have an interest in: Your library reference section can give you assistance. The offices of politicians, especially members of Congress, frequently have this information and will assist you. You can also write to the SBA: U.S. Small Business Administration, 409 Third Street SW, Washington, DC 20416.

A SMALL SPLASH OF COLD WATER

I know this chapter is not a cheering section to learning sales in your own business. I wanted this chapter to be a splash of cold water because being in business may be the most serious step of your life. I think you purchased this book because you want to be among the small 20 percent minority of salespeople and businesspeople who are successful, not in the 80 percent who barely make it.

I haven't pulled any punches. I've told it like it is, the same way I'd explain it to my best friend. The more you understand the rules of the game, the more informed your business decisions will be and the greater your opportunities for real, long-term success. I sincerely want that for you.

17

14 Strategies for Success

This is a series of assorted sales and business strategies I've learned over a period of many years. They come from hard experience and I'm sure you'll find some valuable ideas here.

I tend to believe our success or failure will be the sum total of what we as individuals put into it. For those of us in a highly competitive business market, the ones who put extra effort into their sales and customer strategies will benefit the most. Here's proven ideas to help you accomplish that.

1. Focus on Customers Who Believe in Treating Suppliers Fairly

Some accounts pay only lip service to words like cooperation, partnership, and teamwork. To them, teamwork means "You can have our business as long as you do exactly what we want you to do."

Keep in mind that all buyers are automatically going to demand the lowest possible prices. It's only natural. However, in some organizations, low price is their god. In others, low price is always important, but only so long as good service, product availability, quality, and delivery remain dependable.

Generally (but not always), the larger your customers, the more they are affected by situations other than price. When promises are not kept about quality, delivery, and so on, they have more people involved, more wages and more overhead expenses to pay, and thus more to lose. They are also sophisticated enough to understand that no vendor can be the lowest priced every day, every time, and still provide the service and quality they require. In short, they don't resent you for making a fair profit.

In firms where all you ever hear is, "How cheap can I get that?" there can never be growth because price alone determines customer loyalty. You always have the next guy looking over your shoulder, ready to knock off a few pennies.

While you, of course, will continue to do business with all accounts where you can afford to, your real sales focus should be on new and existing accounts where issues such as quality, availability, delivery, and service are important.

2. Never Tell Your Customer He's King, Then Treat Him Like a Peasant

Everyone promises great service, but few really deliver. Remember, inside every customer complaint is a request for service.

Make sure your telephones are answered professionally, and pleasantly, every time. Make equally sure your customer-service people have people-handling skills. Either train them or change them!

Customer service is meeting or exceeding the customer's expectations. When it comes time to do business again, how do you want people to remember you?

3. Insist Salespeople Use Good Sales-closing Strategies

A recent survey of some 2,000 salespeople revealed some shocking statistics:

50 percent of salespeople will leave a sales interview without asking for an order.

40 percent will ask for an order one time, accept the first resistance, and leave.

Only 10 percent will ask for an order more than once.

No matter how good a talker someone is, any salesperson who can't or won't ask for business, each and every interview, is a drag on your organization. Again, either train them or change them. If you are the salesperson, how do you rate?

4. Eat Lunch with Business Prospects or Customers as Frequently as Possible

One of the most unproductive uses of time is to habitually eat lunch alone, with friends, or employees.

Managers especially often have trouble finding time to visit with accounts, yet the opportunity to communicate in person is critical to building solid relationships. We always have some time for lunch, so why not spend it developing good relations with accounts and people you'd like to do business with? Select one day a week and spend your lunch hour cultivating business relationships with potential clients and existing clients.

I would not go too fancy, in fact, even a fast-food place might be okay for some. Otherwise, people get uncomfortable, thinking you are trying to "buy" their business.

5. Delegate Everything You Possibly Can, Especially the Daily Repetitive Tasks—Find Time to Meet the Long-term Goals of Growth on a Regular Basis

Many of us spend enormous amounts of time each day doing very minor tasks. As a manager, it becomes important that you spend some time devoted to the management, not the daily operation, of the business.

That simply means, as much as possible, delegate to an employee any task you do repeatedly. Forget the thinking that by the time you show someone how to do it, you could have done it yourself. That's the kind of thinking that keeps you trapped forever doing busy work.

Don't fall into the trap of thinking you must orchestrate everyone who does your work. Even if they do it differently than you, so long as it's done okay, leave it be.

Even in a one-person business it's still possible to get help with the everyday tasks. Hire college or high-school students, housewives, retired people, or handicapped people. They often work relatively inexpensively, are usually grateful to find any work at all, and often make very loyal employees. Many have excellent training and work skills. You can hire them on an as-needed basis to keep costs down.

Only when managers focus on the serious issues that only they as managers can handle will the business grow.

> When managers do the work of clerks,
> the company has no manager.

6. Read Sales Books, Listen to Audio Training Tapes, and Enroll in Selling Seminars Whenever Possible

To be really effective, sales training requires repetition. Highly successful salespeople are almost always reading or otherwise studying the art of selling.

Selling is a profession and, as with all successful professions, requires continuous study to excel. Be wary of salespeople who claim they "know that stuff" and don't need to learn anymore. This attitude almost always comes from people who are poor sales performers.

If you are responsible for multiple duties in a small firm or a one-person business, it becomes even more critical that you understand the selling process and practice your skills on a regular basis.

7. Hiring? Watch for Diversity

Watch for individuals with varied backgrounds and multiple talents. One organization hires secretaries and receptionists who double as telemarketers when things slow down. Another firm hires secretaries with accounting experience so they can also double as bookkeepers. One business has the delivery person also doing maintenance work when deliveries are slow. Paying one person $2,000 a month beats paying two people $1,500 a month each.

8. Cash-flow Problems?

Never assume clients expect (or deserve) an open account. Train your salespeople to ask for a deposit. Also, request payment upon delivery or completion of the order. You'll be surprised at how many companies will write you a check on the spot if you simply request it. You also might be surprised to find out how many companies are already doing this successfully in today's tight economy. Don't let salespeople talk you out of this because "you'll lose all your customers." That's just standard flak because you're asking them to do something new and, at the beginning, a little uncomfortable. Most customers will understand and your cash-flow situation won't keep you from sleeping at night.

9. Want Another Cash-flow Idea?

Never plan your finances based on anybody paying within 30 days. Plan on 50 percent paying within 30 to 45 days. Another 30 percent to 40 percent will pay you in the 45-to-60 day range and the balance will pay within 90 days. Somewhere between 1 percent to 5 percent (depending on your business and client mix) will *never* pay. The ones who do pay promptly within 30 days are gold accounts. Treat them accordingly.

10. Low Company Morale?

Be careful how your employees see you. As leader, the image you project carries throughout the organization. Always project a positive, professional image. Leave home problems at home. Keep your business frustrations behind closed office doors. Disagreements should be in private and employees should be disciplined in private. Financial problems are nobody's business but management's. Confidential records need to be locked. Abusive, ill-mannered, or thoughtless behavior by management can destroy a firm.

11. Keep Your Accounting People on Their Toes

While it's very important to respect the training your CPA and/or bookkeeper has, take nothing for granted. Many people, otherwise highly educated, fear to intrude in this area. Nonsense. If you don't comprehend what's going on, the library has plenty of easy-to-understand accounting books for nonaccountants.

Schedule regular meetings to review finances. Spot-check the cash receipts shown on the books with the actual cash received that day. Pull the original invoices for some large accounts at random and see if they match what is shown in the books. Spending 30 minutes a few times a month is a small price to pay to know your books are accurate.

12. Reward Employees with Titles

People place great value on titles. Use titles that will aid your employees in their dealings with the public. In a one-person office, how about Office Manager instead of Secretary? Delivery Manager instead of Driver? Accounting Manager instead of Bookkeeper? If appropriate, have inexpensive business cards printed for them with their name and the new title.

13. Finding the Best Professional Help at Bargain Prices

Often, in a small business, you'll need professional assistance badly, but in a very limited way. When you approach the high-quality professional, the people who are really good at what they do, you can hit a wall two ways.

First, their minimum fees are high, perhaps more than you can afford. You'll find the better professionals are often not interested in small business because their operating overhead is so high they can't afford to take small accounts or one-timers without charging a minimum amount.

Second, if they do take you as a client, because you are small, they don't really value your business. You are not very important in their overall business and you may not get their best work. Complain about something and they may tell you to go elsewhere. They feel they are doing you a favor. They just don't need you.

Following are examples of small jobs that can be difficult to hire top people for on a limited basis. Perhaps an accountant to help you over some rough places as you do your bookkeeping. A graphics artist to design a one-time brochure. A computer expert to help you learn a difficult software program. A writer to prepare a news release or article. A lawyer to review documents. A carpenter to build shelves or remodel an office.

No matter where you live, there are numerous, highly qualified professionals in all kinds of work disciplines who are eager to moonlight. They either have a full-time job and want extra income or may be between jobs. As a moonlighter most do not expect to be paid as high a rate as their full-time employer might pay. The only downside is that some will only be available during nonworking hours or on weekends.

You can find them easily and quickly with an ad in a Sunday classified section. (That's always the most highly read day for job classified ads.) To not waste time, rent a PO box or have the replies go to the newspaper. Ask for and review résumés to make sure they have the background you need. Interview the best and make sure they bring samples of their work (if appropriate) and references to the interview. Be sure to check out the references before hiring. Here's how an ad might look:

> CPA needed part/spare time. Flexible hours. Resume to: PO Box 1234, Yourtown, NY 12345.

14. "When the Fire Is Burning, It's Too Late to Shop for the Best Extinguisher"

If you may need a bank loan in six months or a year, *now* is the time to start meeting with bankers. If you are starting to run out of room for growth at your facility, *now* is the time to start checking out the real-estate market.

Develop a working knowledge of how to locate professional help. Cultivate the acquaintance of professionals when you meet them at business events and social gatherings. Make it a point to ask for their business cards. Find out their areas of specialty, kinds of clients they represent, fees, and so on. Forget that you may have someone you are totally satisfied with. Life plays strange tricks. Nothing lasts forever. People can come and go in both our business and personal lives in a phone call.

Always have business cards in your files of accountants, lawyers, business consultants, real-estate and insurance people who you don't presently do business with but would consider. Do so in advance of catastrophe.

IN CLOSING

Let me reach out across the time and space that separate us to shake your hand. This book is a stepping stone on your journey to success. By the very act of reading it you have indicated your sincere desire for success.

Persistence

Nothing in the world
can take the place of persistence.

Talent will not;
nothing is more common than
unsuccessful people with talent.

Genius will not;
unrewarded genius is almost a proverb.

Education will not;
the world is full of educated derelicts.

Persistence and determination alone
are omnipotent.

Calvin Coolidge
23rd President of the United States

If I can leave you with only one thought, let it be to persevere. I told you early on that whatever business you decide upon, whatever you may be selling, you must firmly believe.

The world is filled with quitters. They are in a majority. Oh sure, they start out strong, they boast and tell others how they plan to succeed, but when problems arise and answers are difficult to find, they start to back off. Anything that isn't easy scares them, although they'll never admit that. They find fault in others and in situations, but they never accept the responsibility for any of their own poor decisions.

Age of the Quick Fix

There's a second problem: People growing up in the age of television. I call it the age of the quick fix. We see TV shows presenting and resolving monumental problems in the span of one hour. We watch the news condense all kinds of human tragedy in a matter of minutes, even seconds, then go on to something totally different.

Watch the interviews on the early-morning network programs or on the news programs. They bring in very interesting people and try to interview them in three or four minutes. Listen to the pace at which the interviewers speak, rapidly so they don't lose anyone's attention.

I gave up listening to most of these programs because they never let the interviewee complete a thought. The answers, if they go past a sentence or two, are cut off. The information is so condensed that often there is confusion about what the interviewee was there for. In the world of television it's called sound bites—that is, short, simple-to-understand, condensed answers.

People watching this, especially young people with little real-world experience, begin to think like that. Problems are solved quickly and we go on to the good stuff.

Real life is just the opposite. Some problems can last a long time, sometimes forever. Solutions are hard to find and even if we do find them, may be even more difficult to implement. The solutions may not be complete, but rather temporary or partial. Many people today have a problem coping. They expect quick and easy solutions. They are always in a hurry to get to the good stuff. When they don't get quick and easy answers, they fold.

Successful businesspeople understand the necessity of working toward solutions. They know there is usually a series of solutions to big problems, not one simple one. They know success is derived from perseverance and hard work.

Being a success in your own business requires you to accept a lot of responsibility for your own personal success. It means you must be willing and able to accept the high risks of failure in order to succeed. It means that when things go wrong, chances are it's your own fault.

Should you beat yourself up for these mistakes? Certainly not, that's nonsense. Not only that, it blocks you from fixing the problem. You can get so down on yourself that you start to feel helpless and give up.

Nobody has all the answers. You simply acknowledge you don't know everything and immediately seek out knowledge from those who do. There's no such thing as a dumb question, but there are a lot of people too foolish to ask questions for fear they'll look dumb.

Finding Help

In my various careers over these many years I always found strength in the fact that I wasn't alone. Whatever problem I was facing, of all the millions and millions of humans who have lived before I got to this point, some, probably many, have faced this identical problem before. What's more, someone somewhere knows how to resolve it. Knowledge surrounds us. It's more accessible in this day and age than ever before in our history.

For years in business my first resource for help was the libraries and bookstores. I learned that there are many great books and tapes from experts in all areas of small business problems, such as sales, accounting, marketing, planning, and so on.

If that didn't cut it I knew that I could get some free advice from SCORE at my local SBA office. I also had a good accountant and attorney I could ask questions of. I knew I could contact successful out-of-town companies in my trade association that actually were not in competition with me and would often give me valuable advice. There were also consultants in my trade association who knew my business very well. Finally, I knew there were business consultants listed in the telephone directory who could also advise me.

The bottom line is I didn't need to spend a lot of time worrying and blaming others about serious business problems. I needed to spend my time productively seeking out answers. If this all sounds simple and easy, please know it's not. It's difficult. It's tough to take on problems and risk, not knowing if you can succeed. But that's what being in business is all about.

The worse things get, the less time you have to panic. Instead, focus on solutions that make sense to you. Even if closing a business is the only real solution, that's not the end of the line. If you ever read biographies of successful men and women in business, almost everyone was in business more than once, with some failures along the way. There's no shame in that. If there were, most of the big, successful firms you see today wouldn't exist.

In a great many cases the biggest problem of small businesses is simply not enough business coming in, a lack of sales. Most of the other problems are a result of low sales. Bring in new business and most other problems are correctable.

This book is designed to assist you in resolving that problem. What I have shared with you over these pages are tried-and-true sales methods that really do work. Learn them and use them.

I'm aware that I've repeated myself and my advice may be a little harsh in spots. I did this to emphasize critical areas because I want you to succeed. I want you to use this book to achieve whatever your business goals may be. I know it may be a little difficult in the beginning, but please make the effort. The results can make a huge difference in your life.

I saw a movie whose title I have forgotten, but not this wonderful quote. Someone turned to the hero and said, "Gee, this is really hard! Isn't there an easy way?"

The hero's response was, "Of course not. If there were, everybody would be doing it! Just think how special you'll be and how great you'll feel when you make it!"

My sincere best wishes to you in your future endeavors.

Good luck and good selling!

Appendix

A

Time Management Resources

There are numerous kinds of time-management tools, from scheduling boards to pocket appointment books. They are not all the same. Each has its own approach to how time can be managed. The trick to being happy using them is to select one that fits your needs and personality. I'd suggest looking at a few different ones before making a final decision. It does not need to be expensive; the more simple the system, the more you will tend to use it.

In addition, there are several computer software programs available that also allow you to track appointments, phone calls, and to-do's. They are called contact software programs. If you are a salesperson, however, unless you have a portable computer, these programs are limited to use at your office. A program called ACT and another from Daytimers are receiving good reviews. Keep in mind that this is a rapidly changing field and new programs are being released constantly.

I strongly recommend that you read the reviews of computer software in the leading PC magazines, available at newsstands or your library, before you invest. It's best to spend a little time investigating what's available instead of grabbing the first thing you see. You can write or telephone any of these firms listed here and they will send you a catalog showing their various time-management systems.

Caddylak
510 Fillmore Avenue
Tonawanda, NY 14150
Telephone 800-523-8060
Fax 800-222-1934

Daytimers
One Daytimer Plaza
Allentown, PA 18195-1551
Telephone 800-225-5384

Franklin Quest
2200 West Parkway Boulevard
Salt Lake City, UT 84119-2331
Telephone 800-654-1776
Fax 800-242-1492

Time Design
265 Main Street
Agawam, MA 01001
Telephone 800-637-9942
Fax 800-269-3075

Time Resources
239 Littleton Road
Westford, MA 01886
Telephone 800-358-8463
Fax 800-437-3150

U.S. Diary Company
One U.S. Diary Center
Bannockburn, IL 60015-1576
Telephone 708 -948-8190
Fax 708-948-0387

Appendix

B

Telemarketer's Dictionary

Appointment: When you get a decision maker to agree to a specific time and day for you to stop by and discuss your product or services.

Boiler Room: Outdated term for room filled with salespeople making telemarketing calls.

Completed Call: When your call results in your speaking with a decision maker, regardless of what the decision maker says to you.

Decision Maker: The person who has the authority to make a buying decision.

Dial: When you dial the correct number, the phone rings and somebody, not necessarily your suspect, picks up the phone and says "Hello."

Dialing for Dollars: Old term used before pushbutton telephones to indicate someone telemarketing.

Gatekeeper: A third party who intercepts calls for decision makers. Frequently a secretary or receptionist in a business; a spouse when calling residential phone numbers.

Prospect: A suspect who has been qualified as having some degree of initial interest and ability to buy.

Suspect: A person who may be a prospect but has not been qualified.

Telephone Solicitor: Old term for telemarketer.

Visit: When a decision maker actually sits down with you. (Sometimes referred to as a completed appointment sitdown or sit.)

Appendix
C

Desktop Publishing Resources

Why bother to send away for catalogs of desktop publishing supplies when many large retail firms sell them? Unfortunately, as retailers become larger and larger, they tend to stock only items they can sell quickly, and their choices are very limited. Catalog merchandisers, however, will feature a much broader selection and carry products not often found in retail stores. It's just good business to know what's available. The following firms will send you a catalog of many clever preprinted forms, software, and desktop publishing supplies.

Some of the companies have more than one catalog and, if so, I have indicated the name of the catalog to request for these items. I have used the toll-free numbers whenever they were given. While this list has been checked for accuracy when it was written, remember, firms go out of business, merge, or move.

Baudville
5380 52nd Street, SE
Grand Rapids, MI 49512-9765
Telephone 800-728-0888
Fax 616-698-0554

Great Papers
PO Box 8465
Mankato, MN 56002-8465
Telephone 800-287-8163
Fax 800-842-3371

Idea Art
PO Box 291505
Nashville, TN 37229-1505
Telephone 800-433-2278
Fax 800-435-2278

Moore Business Forms
(Image Street catalog)
PO Box 5000
Vernon Hills, IL 60061
Telephone 800-462-4378 0149
Fax 800-329-6667

NEBS, Inc.
(Computer forms
and software catalog)
500 Main Street
Groton, MA 01471
Telephone 800-225-9550
Fax 800-234-4324

On Paper
PO Box 1365
Elk Grove Village, IL 60009-1365
Telephone 800-820-2299
Fax 708-595-2094

Paper Direct
PO Box 1514
Secaucus, NJ 07096-1514
Telephone 800-272-7377
Fax 800-443-2973

Quill Corporation
(Laser and Inkjet
Supplies catalog)
100 Schelter Road
Lincolnshire, IL 60069-3621
Telephone 800-789-5813
Fax 800-789-8955

Reliable Office Supplies
1001 W. Van Buren Street
Chicago, IL 60607
Telephone 800-735-4000
Fax 800-326-3233

The Stationery House
(Queblo catalog)
1000 Florida Avenue
Hagerstown, MD 21741
Telephone 800-523-9080
Fax 800-554-8779

Tiger Software
(Graphics Express catalog)
Suite 1200
9100 S. Dadeland Boulevard
Miami, FL 33156
Telephone 800-335-4054
Fax 305-529-2990

Appendix
D
Government Information

To use the SBA on-line telephone number, you'll need a computer with a communications software package installed (which is usually included when you buy a telephone modem). The listing bps means bits per second and refers to the transmission speed of a modem. You need a modem whose fastest speed matches the on-line service. For instance, if your modem is rated at 2,400 bps, you can contact a bulletin board whose speed is 1,200 or 2,400, but not one that is rated at 9,600 bps.

The 800 SBA phone number is toll-free. A good time to call is late in the evenings and/or weekends, when fewer people are using the services and connections are much easier.

SBA On-line: 2,400bps—800-859-4636; 9,600 bps—800-697-4636

SCORE Program: The telephone number for the national SCORE office is 800-634-0245; fax 202-205-7636. They can put you in contact with an office near you.

SBA offices: For information on contacting an SBA office near you or other SBA information, call: The Small Business Answer Desk at 800-827-5722 or fax 202-205-7333. I suggest you also request a copy of their booklet, *The Small Business Directory*. It is free, and it lists their business development publications and products.

The States and Small Business: A Directory of Programs and Activities: Published by The Office of Advocacy, U.S. Small Business Administration. The brochure I have is the 1993 edition, which shows an order #045-000-00266-7. You can order from the Superintendent of Documents, Washington, DC, but first check if an updated issue is available. There is a charge for this publication.

Appendix

E

Miscellaneous

Tate & Associates
PO Box 954-W
Mentor, OH 44016-0954

Consultants, Seminars, Workshops, Speeches,

Sales training audio tapes,

Motiviational miniposters,

Time-management forms

Index

C